More Praise for *Talent Intelligence*

"Attracting, selecting, and retaining the right talent is a critical competitive edge for organizations today. In this sometimes shocking and eminently useful book, the authors lay out some of the challenges and complexities of talent measurement and show how by choosing the right combination of methods and tools—and implementing them consistently—businesses can produce good talent intelligence."
— **Dr. Nandani Lynton**, leadership development director,
A.P. Møller - Mærsk A/S

"Practical and provocative, this book provides a clear and comprehensive road map for cutting through the complexity and myths surrounding talent measurement. Essential reading for all HR professionals who want clear guidance on what to measure, how to measure it, and most importantly how to turn the data into genuine talent intelligence."
— **Ryan Eagar**, Global Learning and Development,
HEINEKEN International

"This book is revelatory—it challenges commonly held beliefs about talent measurement and clarifies what is and is not possible. It will change the way you think about what you do."
— **Alan Arnett**, head of Talent Development, XL Group

"This book is essential reading for all HR professionals and managers who care about the management of talent in their organizations. It is a highly practical guide to talent measurement that makes this complex subject easy to understand and more possible to implement."
— **Martin Jahn**, head of Global Fleet Sales, Volkswagen AG

"This intelligent book resets all assumptions and expectations about talent measurement and shows how businesses can better identify truly global potential in individuals in our search for an Asian way to corporate globalization."

—**Toyohiro Matsuda**, head of Human Resources Development Asia, Mitsubishi Corporation

"In this highly accessible and useful guide to finding and evaluating talent, the authors have succeeded in simplifying the science of measuring talent for business readers. Although grounded in research, the book avoids much of the jargon typically found in research literature and focuses on what is most relevant to companies trying to identify talent. The authors summarize what works and what does not, highlight the problems associated with measurement tools, and offer practical and clear advice on how to approach this daunting task."

—**Nancy Tippins**, senior VP, CEB Valtera; past president of the American Psychological Association's Organizational/ Industrial Psychology Division

"This compelling book brings a scientific and systematic approach to a critical but previously underdeveloped element of talent management—namely, how organizations can make sure that the people they are hiring, retaining, and promoting are the best ones for their business. Arguing that companies cannot just leave this issue to chance or the natural skills of their managers, the authors show how firms can achieve a real competitive advantage in the talent market through a more sophisticated and effective approach to talent measurement. Informative, enlightening, and essential reading for business and human resources leaders."

—**Jackie Wong**, executive director and CEO, Temasek Management Services

Talent Intelligence

Talent Intelligence

What You Need to Know to Identify and Measure Talent

Nik Kinley

Shlomo Ben-Hur

JB JOSSEY-BASS™
A Wiley Brand

Cover image: Thinkstock
Cover design: Adrian Morgan

Published by Jossey-Bass
A Wiley Brand
One Montgomery Street, Suite 1200, San Francisco, CA 94104-4594—www.josseybass.com

Jossey-Bass books and products are available through most bookstores. To contact Jossey-Bass directly call our Customer Care Department within the U.S. at 800-956-7739, outside the U.S. at 317-572-3986, or fax 317-572-4002.

Wiley publishes in a variety of print and electronic formats and by print-on-demand. Some material included with standard print versions of this book may not be included in e-books or in print-on-demand. If this book refers to media such as a CD or DVD that is not included in the version you purchased, you may download this material at http://booksupport.wiley.com. For more information about Wiley products, visit www.wiley.com.

Library of Congress Cataloging-in-Publication Data
Kinley, Nik, date.
  Talent intelligence : what you need to know to identify and measure talent / Nik Kinley, Shlomo Ben-Hur. – First edition.
      pages cm
  Includes bibliographical references and index.
  ISBN 978-1-118-53118-1 (cloth); ISBN 978-1-118-64008-1 (ebk); ISBN 978-1-118-64028-9 (ebk); 978-1-118-64007-4 (ebk)
  1. Personnel management.   2. Employees–Rating of.   3. Employees–Recruiting.
I. Ben-Hur, Shlomo, 1962– II. Title.
  HF5549.K4994 2013
  658.3'01–dc23
                              2013007356

Printed in the United States of America

FIRST EDITION

HB Printing   10 9 8 7 6 5 4 3 2 1

To Connie, for her love and support.
For keeping the world turning while I wrote this.
And to Lukas, for his patience and for reminding me that
there are other things than writing books.
Yes, Papa can play now.—N.K.

*   *   *

To my beloved sisters Orly, Yula, and Inbar,
each talented in her own very special way.—S.B.H.

Contents

Acknowledgments

As with any other such undertaking, many people have contributed to this book. There are some without whom this book would never have happened. There are others who have helped us develop our thinking and form our ideas, both recently and over the years. And then there are those who have helped us write and hone the text. It is a long list, and we are grateful to them all.

Unfortunately, there is not enough space to name everyone, but there are some we absolutely must mention—people who have directly contributed time and effort to help us write this. At the top of this list has to be Lindsay McTeague, our brilliant copyeditor at IMD, and the fantastic Kathe Sweeney, Alina Poniewaz, Bev Miller, Carol Hartland, and Alan Venable at Jossey-Bass. Then, in alphabetical order, are Alan Arnett, Laurence Barrett, John Bassett, Georg Bauer, Stephanie Bird, Bill Byham, Jacqueline Davies, Ryan Eagar, Samantha Halverson, Peter Hartmann, Helen Hopper, Christopher Howarth, Martin Jahn, Fiona Laing, David Lawton, Andrew Lopianowski, Nandani Lynton, Rab MacIver, Mikkel Madvig, Farzana Maudarbaccus, Laura McKeaveney, Shauna McVeigh, Gabby Parry, Eyal Pavel, Elisabeth Pircher, David Ringwood, Peter Saville, Robert Sharrock, Nancy Tippins, Caroline Vanovermeire, and Jackie Wong.

About the Authors

Nik Kinley is a London-based independent consultant who has specialized in the fields of measurement and behavior change for over twenty years. He has worked with CEOs, factory-floor workers, life-sentence prisoners, government officials, and children. His prior roles include global head of assessment for the BP Group, head of learning for Barclays GRBF, and senior consultant with YSC, the leading European assessment and development consultancy.

He began his career in commercial roles, before spending the next decade working in forensic psychotherapy. Ten years ago, he returned to working with organizations and since then has worked with over half of the top twenty FTSE companies, identifying and developing talent across the globe. He now specializes in consulting with businesses to help them build their talent intelligence and enhance the performance of their people, and consulting with vendors to help them develop talent and learning-related products and services. He holds a master's degree in systemic psychotherapy and a bachelor's degree in psychology from the University of London.

*　　*　　*

Shlomo Ben-Hur is an organizational psychologist and a professor of leadership and organizational behavior at IMD business school in Lausanne, Switzerland. His areas of focus are the psychological and cultural aspects of leadership and the strategic and operational elements of talent management and corporate learning. In addition to teaching leadership on two of IMD's top programs for senior executives, he creates programs for and consults with a wide variety of organizations across the globe.

Prior to joining IMD, he spent twenty years in the corporate world, most recently as vice president of leadership development and learning for the BP Group based in London and earlier as chief learning officer of DaimlerChrysler Services AG in Berlin. He earned his doctoral degree in psychology from the Humboldt University of Berlin. He holds a master's degree in industrial/organizational psychology and a bachelor's degree in psychology and political science from Bar-Ilan University in Israel.

*   *   *

Contact the authors at inbox@measuringtalent.com or check out their blog with the latest news, information, and advice on talent intelligence at www.measuringtalent.com.

Talent Intelligence

1

TALENT MEASUREMENT

Is It Measuring Up?

The challenge with most companies' talent intelligence is that it is just not that intelligent.

Having good talent intelligence—an accurate understanding of the skills, expertise, and qualities of people—is essential for the people decisions that every business makes. If they are to avoid randomly hiring and promoting people, all companies need to evaluate and gauge individuals' talents. It is a basic and fundamental task, one that every manager and organization does, and one that everyone agrees needs to be done well. Yet all the available evidence suggests that it is not.

The reason lies in talent measurement—how organizations go about gathering and using information about the talents of their people—because it seems that this crucial task is often taken for granted, not well understood, or undertaken in ways that limit its value to firms.

This book is about why this is so, what has gone wrong, and what organizations can do to rectify the matter. And they do need to rectify it because the world is changing in ways that mean they will no longer be able to get away with not doing it well. To thrive in the coming decades, firms are going to need good talent intelligence, and they are going to need to use it in ways that deliver real value and competitive advantage for them. And to achieve this, they are going to have to get talent measurement right. The good news is that they can.

The Hidden Role of Talent Measurement

Talent measurement is the use of various methods and tools to gather and use information about individuals' talents. There is no one way of doing it. Some organizations rely on the intuition of their leaders and simple interviews; others employ sophisticated online tests. Both, though, have the same purpose: to identify whether job applicants and current employees have the abilities, expertise, and characteristics they need to help both them and their businesses thrive and be successful.

As a task, talent measurement is often hidden away, part of bigger and broader processes. Yet it is there. It is key to recruitment, promotion, high-flier identification, restructuring layoffs, organizational design, individual development, competence assurance in technical roles, and due diligence for mergers and acquisitions.

Unsung it may be, but talent measurement is a fundamental foundation of modern talent management. It is a basic building block in successfully managing workforces, helping identify who adds value right now, and who could do so going forward. And although it may have been a low-profile activity to date, it is about to have its day in the sun.

Why Talent Measurement Matters More Than Ever Before

Talent management is changing, and as it does so, it is leading businesses increasingly to focus and rely on talent measurement.

Almost fifteen years ago, McKinsey declared that a "war for talent" was coming, and it seems they got it right.[1] Globalization and shifting population demographics are causing competition for talent to rise steadily and persistently and making it harder than ever before for businesses to find the talent they need.

In the West, only 18 percent of firms say they have enough talent in place to meet future business needs, and more than half report that their business is already being held back by a lack of leadership talent.[2] Worryingly, 75 percent of businesses report difficulty in filling vacancies too.[3] The temporary increase in available workers created by the downturn is not helping either, as there is evidence that all the choice is making it more difficult to spot the best people.[4]

The situation is generally not as critical in emerging markets, but this will change. In China, for example, the predominantly manufacturing base of its economy has largely protected it from these concerns up to now. Yet as service industries and the use of knowledge workers grow and the impact of the country's one-child policy is felt, China too will face these challenges. The war for talent is going global.

It is not actual war, of course, but there will be casualties and there will be winners. We know that businesses that are better at talent management and better able to find and keep the best people tend to outperform their industry's average return to shareholders by around 22 percent.[5] In fact, making good hiring and promotion decisions can have a bigger impact on market value than creating a customer-focused environment, improving benefits, or having good union relationships.[6] And amid stronger competition for talent, these performance advantages for companies that are effective at identifying and managing talent are likely to increase.

Realizing this, alert organizations are turning to talent management for solutions and investing in it too A recent U.S. Department of Labor report predicted that over the next ten years, the number of people in human resources (HR) and talent management professions will grow at more than double the rate of the general workforce.[7]

Driven by all this attention and investment, talent management is changing. Perhaps most notable, and arguably long overdue, it is becoming far more data led. People data have become currency, and *workforce analytics* is the buzzword of the moment. The idea is simple and compelling: to manage talent and make good personnel decisions requires knowing what you need, what you have, and what is available. And to make this possible, new software systems have emerged that promise to help you gather, manage, and use talent information more effectively than ever before.

You might assume that talent measurement would be at the heart of this analytical talent management revolution, but, oddly, this has not typically been the case so far. Instead, these talent systems tend to use data such as demographics and distributions—that is, workforce composition. This type of administrative information does have uses, but it is limited in terms of what you can do with it and the value you can add with it. So while many of these new talent management tools are undeniably impressive, they are, like all other systems, only as good as the data you put into them. And in this respect, they are lacking.

A few larger companies have sought to rectify this by putting talent measurement at the heart of these systems. Google, predictably, is ahead of the curve when it comes to people data. Unsure of whether it was hiring the best applicants, the company started developing a comprehensive database that captured information about current employees' attitudes, behaviors, personality, biographical information, and job performance. This database has allowed Google to develop an algorithm for predicting which applicants are most likely to succeed at the company.[8] It is too early to judge how effective the algorithm is, and this kind of approach would not be suitable for all businesses. Yet it is clearly more sophisticated in its approach than mere demographics and has the potential to yield far more value.

Other organizations are following suit. For example, a major UK retail bank recently linked the results of its employee engagement survey to administrative data on people, measurement data, and customer service feedback scores for individual bank branches. As a result, it was better able to understand what the business and branch managers needed to do to improve the customer experience.

So businesses are beginning to realize the potential of measuring talent systematically and combining talent data with other information to produce insights of real business value. This may sound like good news and a great opportunity. And it is. But it can be seized as an opportunity only if talent measurement works and produces good-quality intelligence, which is where things get worrying.

The Ineffectiveness of Most Talent Measurement

Unfortunately, the vast majority of organizations are ineffective in how they measure talent. Even among companies that are measuring talent effectively, most are using the information it provides in ways that mean they derive only a small margin of the real value it can deliver.

For example, surveys show that less than one-third of business leaders rate their company's selection processes as effective.[9] Indeed, while they see selection as the most important task of talent management, they also view it as the least effective.[10] This is not limited to just hiring either. The results for other talent identification processes—such as promoting, benchmarking, or identifying potential future leaders—are not much better. This may be hard to hear, and your first instinct may be to dismiss it or rationalize it away. But it gets worse.

Over the past thirty years, businesses have invested heavily in trying to find the best people, to the extent that this period has witnessed the development of a global talent identification industry. There is the corporate recruitment market—the headhunting firms whose collected annual revenues prior to the downturn were estimated to be in excess of US$10 billion worldwide. And then there is the specialist talent measurement market, estimated to be worth more than US$3 billion per annum globally.

With all this investment, you might expect to find that businesses had significantly improved their ability to identify talent and hire the right people. Yet when we compare research from thirty years ago into how well new employees do with research from today, this is not what we find. Instead, the rate of failure among new employees seems to have risen. Thirty years ago, it was estimated that about one-third of all new employees failed.[11] Today, reported failure rates range from 30 to 67 percent, with an average of about 50 percent.[12]

What is shocking about this is not so much the high rate of failure or even the rise in failure rates over the past few decades, but that the measurement industry has had no discernible impact on these rates. Somehow, despite massive investment in measurement and the widespread adoption of sophisticated methods and tools, we do not appear to have achieved meaningful improvements in failure rates. There is no shortage of case studies showcasing individual organizations that have done great work in this area, but across the board, this success is just not shared.

In almost any other area of business, investing that kind of money and not making a dent in failure rates would be unacceptable—or at least it should be. As a number of commentators have noted, in a world where organizations are placing an unerring focus on results, they seem to tolerate surprisingly low success rates when it comes to hiring and promoting people.[13] Indeed, it is hard to think of any other area of management where such poor performance would be tolerated.[14]

That is not to say that the task is easy. The sheer complexity and number of variables involved is often understated, and some of the reasons and circumstances that cause people to fail are not predictable.[15] For this reason, we are unlikely ever to reach 90 percent of our people decisions being highly effective. But we should be doing better than we are.

So what is going on? One obvious possibility that springs to mind is that current talent measurement methods do not work or even that "talent" cannot be measured. But decades of research have unequivocally demonstrated that some measurement methods and tools are better at predicting both overall performance and individual elements of it than the traditional, basic selection procedure of using just unstructured interviews.[16] In fact, study after study has driven this point home until it is no longer a matter of debate. Moreover, if accurate talent measurement were not possible, then no one would be making any progress. But that is not what we see. Instead, there appear to be pockets of excellence surrounded by a general lack of progress.

Studies show, for example, that effective talent measurement in recruitment and promotion processes can lead to reduced turnover, improved performance levels, and faster integration and time to full productivity. Indeed, effective talent measurement in hiring executives has been shown to result in companies being eight times more likely to hire someone they keep and go on to later promote.[17] And it is not just success rates that good measurement can have an impact on. The use of some measurement tools has been shown to be able to cut absenteeism and decrease both accidents at work and employee theft.

So measurement *can* work and the growing use of it over the past thirty years should have had a greater impact. Somehow, somewhere, something has gone wrong. And it is a critical issue, because if businesses cannot make talent measurement work, the rest of their talent management activities are likely to come up short.

Why Talent Measurement Is Not Working

In our work with organizations around the world looking at the issues they face in talent measurement, we have found five common challenges:

1. Talent measurement is unavoidably complex.
2. It is hard to know what works.
3. Measurement methods do not always meet business needs.
4. Implementation gets overlooked.
5. Businesses lack expertise.

Each challenge by itself can significantly limit the ability of measurement to have the sort of impact we would expect. But in our experience, most organizations are struggling on all five fronts.

Talent Measurement Is Unavoidably Complex

It is difficult to do something well if you do not fully understand it, and talent measurement is a highly technical business. Indeed, it has its own subareas of expertise, such as the mathematics of test design, which many measurement professionals themselves do not fully understand. Not everyone needs to know all the technical details, of course, but even at an operational level, measurement can be complex.

For starters, you need to know what you want to measure. Companies usually know this at a broad level—for example, they want to know if someone is a potential leader for the future. Yet knowing what specifically to measure can be a lot harder. Is it behavioral competencies and, if so, which ones? Should you look for intelligence? Personality? Ambition? And how do you know which qualities make the biggest difference in which situations?

Moreover, what if the best test to use in order to predict future performance also happens to be the one that shows most bias against some racial groups? Or what if an organization wants to use one consistent measurement tool across all its offices around the world, but some countries have regulations controlling which measures can be used? These, in fact, are some of the most common complexities that businesses encounter, and they can create significant problems.

The complexity does not end once you have worked out what to measure. You then have to choose the right tool for the task, and here you encounter the thorny issue of how to ensure that you are accurately measuring what you set out to assess. For example, we encountered a major global bank that in its Singapore office used a respected test to assess the intelligence of all job applicants. Yet it was assessing all of the candidates, no matter what their background, using tests written in English. The logic was simple enough: it wanted to be able to benchmark candidates' intelligence with that of people in the UK head office. The complexity the firm did not grasp, however, was that it was not getting a true, accurate reading of intelligence because candidates' language abilities were affecting how well they did on the test. What the company should have done was to use intelligence tests in candidates' native language, and if it wanted to assess their English ability as well, then it should have also administered a separate language skills test.

Of course, complexity in itself is not a problem. It becomes problematic only when the complexity is not recognized or is underestimated. So it is unfortunate that many vendors, in an effort not to scare potential customers away, tend to downplay the complexities and keep the inner workings of measurement out of sight. It is commercially understandable and, from a customer's viewpoint possibly, preferable. After all, we live in a world in which convenience, keeping things simple, and "just-do-it" solutions are valued. But understanding complexity can sometimes be necessary for things to work effectively, and this is certainly true for measurement. Measurement *is* a complex issue, and if it is to be done well, it needs to be treated as such. Failure to do so will mean that whatever you do, the chances are it will not work.

It Is Hard to Know What Works

Adding to the complexity is the fact that finding the right solution can be difficult. The measurement market is awash with a mass of different methods and tools, and the choice can be bewildering. Information about which tools should be used when and which work best tends to come from one of three sources:

1. *Academic researchers*—who are not always interested in the same issues as organizations and whose findings often need translation for nonacademic readers

2. *Vendors*—whose commoditization of measurement methods creates a conflict of interest in terms of objectively reporting their efficacy

3. *Colleagues in other organizations*—whose interests, like those of the vendors, are not served by reporting negative findings

In theory the best source of information should be academic research because it is the only reliably objective source. Yet surveys show that HR professionals and business leaders alike rarely read academic journals and often consider research contradictory or irrelevant.[18] And who can blame them? The research literature can be hard to access and even harder to understand. As preparation for this book, we read over a thousand articles, so with some authority, we can confirm that they can be difficult to understand and downright mind numbing.

The result is that businesses tend to be relatively uninformed about measurement research and have to rely instead on what vendors tell them. Yet without objective sources of information, HR and business leaders often report feeling intimidated by the apparent expertise of vendors—or at least unable to question or challenge what vendors tell them.

The importance of this is that organizations need to question and challenge what they hear. Some excellent vendors, services, and tools are on the market, but there are estimated to be over two thousand test publishers in the United States alone, and only a minority of them engages in any proper validity studies.[19] So only a small percentage of vendors can say with any objective authority that they know that their measurement methods genuinely work.

Moreover, even when they do have evidence of the quality of their tools, this information cannot be taken at face value.

The reason lies in the worrying trend of reporting bias: the tendency for people to publish only positive results or ones that further their arguments or products. Measurement is, of course, a business, and we understand that in this commercial environment, vendors need to present themselves well. But recent research shows that reporting bias is far more prevalent than you might expect in an industry that professes to be grounded in science.

At a broad level, for example, there is evidence that academic research findings are less favorable about the success of measurement than research produced by vendors.[20] More specifically, studies have identified reporting bias by some very well-known psychometric test publishers.[21] The publisher of one of the most globally used personality tests, for instance, states that the tool has great validity, yet a review by a respected independent body has concluded that "the test suffers from questionable reliability and unknown validity. Its use is not recommended."[22]

Probably the most public example of the issue is the tale of emotional intelligence. In the mid-1990s psychologist and author Daniel Goleman brought to the fore the idea that emotional skills are important for leadership success. On the back of the book came a number of tools claiming to measure emotional intelligence, and with them came claims that they could account for 80 percent of the factors that determine success.

Almost twenty years on, however, there is now overwhelming independent research showing that emotional intelligence measures are actually some of the less effective predictors of success. This does not mean that emotional intelligence is not important for leadership. It simply means that measures of it are nowhere near as good at predicting success as initially claimed. Yet if you Google these measures, you will find the same original weighty claims still being made by some big-name vendors selling them, without mention of the decades' worth of independent research findings to the contrary.[23]

This prevalence of biased validity figures makes the recent actions of one of the biggest test providers in the world all the more concerning. It appears to have changed its contractual terms to prevent independent research into the validity of its tests without its approval and permission. In our view, this throws any kind of pretense about objective science straight out of the window.

So not only is measurement a complex, technical, and all-too-often impenetrable field, but knowing who and what to trust is not easy. Little wonder that when recently asking for our help in setting up a new talent measurement process, one of the biggest companies in the world said that it felt "vulnerable" to the market.

It may feel at this point that there is no easy way to determine if measures and tools actually work. But all you need to know is which questions to ask and what to look out for in the answers. And businesses have the opportunity here not just to find out which tools work, but also to change how the measurement market works and make it easier to navigate. For example, if they stop using vendors who do not provide proper validity information, those vendors will either start producing it or disappear. And if firms simply refuse to use vendors that prohibit independent research into their tools, then these vendors will soon revert to allowing it. Far from being hopeless, the reality of the situation is that armed with just a little knowledge, you can make a big difference.

Measurement Methods Do Not Always Meet Business Needs

The choice of what measures and tools to use is complicated by the fact that they have traditionally been developed without considering how organizations use them. As a result, researchers and vendors have sometimes developed measurement methods that look great in theory and are strongly able to predict performance, but have not been used or are not much liked by businesses.

The biggest example of this can be seen in the academic articles expressing surprise that businesses so frequently ignore one of the most accepted findings in measurement research: that structured interviews tend to be far better able to predict performance than unstructured interviews. This surprise betrays a lack of understanding that the purpose of interviews for businesses is not just to predict performance. Interviews also need to leave candidates with a positive impression of the company and give managers a chance to gauge what their working relationship with candidates might be like. Yet proposals to heavily structure interviews, which in the strictest sense does not allow for any unscripted questions, clearly do not acknowledge these additional objectives. Some researchers have suggested that the reason structured interviews are not used more is that their benefits have not been clearly communicated.[24] The reality is that they simply do not meet business needs.

Furthermore, researchers and test developers for the most part have taken the objective of measurement to be predicting job performance. At present, the yardstick for whether a measure is viewed as valid or effective is if it can predict who receives the best overall performance ratings. This certainly sounds reasonable, and indeed it is, in that this kind of information can be important in making people decisions. Yet the emphasis on predicting performance has been so strong that it has come at the expense of also trying to develop tools that can predict other factors that may affect a person's success.

For example, hiring managers are usually not only interested in who is the most able or could theoretically perform best. They also tend to be interested in factors such as whether potential new employees will get along with them, fit with the company's values, or work well with their coworkers. These issues may not sound as immediately compelling as candidates' likely overall level of performance. Nevertheless, they are critical to individuals' longer-term success and are some of the most frequent reasons people eventually "fail" in a role, despite considerable apparent ability. Let's face it: if your manager does not like you, then chances are that you are not going to succeed no matter how good you are on paper.

To be fair, there has been a shift in recent years. Vendors are beginning to produce more user-friendly tools and are starting to look at a broader range of factors that lead to success. And, of course, some vendors are better at this than others. But in general, the move has been late, slow, and minimal, and it has some way to go.

Implementation Gets Overlooked

Knowing what to measure and how to measure it may be the most obvious challenges facing businesses when it comes to gauging talent, but they are not the biggest ones. In fact, in spite of everything we have said about how hard it is to know what works, the choice of measurement processes is usually the easiest thing to get right. It is everything else that is much harder for businesses to do effectively—things such as how they use measurement outputs to make decisions, how well they integrate measurement activities with other processes, and the degree to which they use measurement data to inform their broader people strategy.

The importance of these implementation issues is that if insufficient attention is paid to them, they can fundamentally limit the value and usefulness of the intelligence that talent measurement produces. Yet insufficient attention is exactly what these issues typically receive.

Working both within organizations and as external consultants to them, we have lost count of the number of times we have been asked to help set up a new measurement process or identify the best tool to use. But rarely have we been asked about how to make more use of measurement data or how to develop a company's attitudes and approach to using the data. Yet in our experience, it is such seemingly peripheral issues that all too often constrain and limit the potential impact and value of measurement processes.

For example, one of the easiest wins with measurement data collected in recruitment processes is to use this information to help tailor initial developmental support for new joiners. Yet research shows that only 19 percent of firms do this.[25] It is certainly common enough to hear talk of how important such issues are, but the reality is that all too often, they are an afterthought and so not implemented effectively, if at all.

The shame in all of this is that measurement can do so much more than merely guide and support individual people decisions and development. Indeed, not doing more with the results is probably the single biggest missed opportunity that exists with measurement. With the advent of talent analytics, the situation is changing as businesses look more closely at what they can use measurement data for, but they have a lot of catching up to do.

Businesses Lack Expertise

Finally, to meet the first four challenges successfully, you either need to have measurement expertise yourself or access to someone who does. Unfortunately, the people who make decisions about measurement issues and manage vendors frequently have little such expertise themselves and little independent expertise available to them.[26] As a result, they often either use the wrong measurement processes for their needs or use them in ways that limit their impact.

An increasing number of companies do employ experts to help them navigate the market and manage processes. Yet these roles are typically at a fairly junior level and predominantly tactical in nature. As a result, they can have little influence on measurement strategy. Of course, many smaller firms cannot afford or justify employing specialists and so have to find and rely on external experts and vendors. In itself, there is nothing wrong with this. But with little knowledge of the field, it is not easy to be effective in choosing and managing vendors.

In an effort to navigate the field, firms often resort to what Peter Saville, one of the fathers of modern measurement, calls *faith validity*. This is the tendency to become attached to particular tests or vendors that are familiar instead of objectively considering what works best.[27] Yet surveys show a large diversity of opinion among HR professionals on which measurement methods work best.[28] And wide gaps appear to exist between what research tells us is the best approach and what practitioners and businesses believe and in fact do.[29]

For example, the highly popular Myers-Briggs Type Indicator (MBTI) continues to be used in selection processes, even though the test distributors repeatedly assert that it should not be applied in this context.[30] As a more general example, there is the continued use of graphology in places like France despite a mass of evidence demonstrating its lack of efficacy.[31] And we recently came across a business that claimed that the measure it used to help identify which candidates to hire was right 95 percent of the time. Yet this belief in the tool appears to be unfounded. The company has never evaluated it, and in the tool's technical manual, the vendor suggests that it could account for only 3 percent of the reasons that people succeed. Something does not add up.

This is not to say that businesses need to know everything about measurement—far from it. Of course, the more access to expertise they have, the better. But we are convinced that even smaller firms without access to independent expertise can successfully manage measurement and make it work for them. All they need is a basic understanding of the challenges, knowledge of what fundamental questions they should always ask, and an awareness of how they can make the most of measurement.

The Purpose of This Book

From these five issues, it is obvious why getting measurement right can be difficult and why both measurement and the talent intelligence it produces appears to be having little impact.

The purpose of this book is to show how organizations can overcome these challenges. It is thus not about how to do measurement—how to run an interview or the various algorithms for sifting candidates. It is about how to implement measurement in ways that produce good talent intelligence and have a genuine impact on the bottom line.

Moreover, one of the key messages of this book is that the solutions required to make measurement work lie within organizations. As much as vendors are trying to produce and promote shinier, shorter, and smarter new tools and tests, it is organizations that hold the key to progress. In fact, there are some simple things that all businesses can do that have the potential to transform the efficacy of talent measurement and thus the quality of their talent intelligence.

In the chapters that follow, we guide you through the three basic things that businesses need to know and get right to make measurement work:

- They need to know what to measure.
- They need to know how to measure it.
- They need to know how to implement measurement and use the results.

Chapters 2 and 3 are all about what to measure. We begin in chapter 2 by looking at the standard measures of talent—some of the common factors that businesses look at to try and gauge people's talent—things like experience, competencies, intelligence, and personality. And we present an accessible summary of what the very latest research has to say about which—if any—of these factors can genuinely be used to identify talent. In chapter 3, we explore some simple things that all firms can do to dramatically improve their chances of accurately predicting who is most likely to succeed.

Chapters 4 and 5 are about how to measure. Chapter 4 describes the various methods and tools that can be used, and chapter 5 focuses on how businesses can best choose which to use: the basics they need to know and the questions they need to ask.

Chapters 6, 7, and 8 are about how to implement talent measurement and use the results. In chapter 6, we look at the foundations that talent measurement needs to be built on to be effective—the things that need to be in place for it to have the impact it should. Chapter 7 is about how companies can ensure that the output of measurement, the intelligence provided, is used to best effect. And in chapter 8, we go on to explore how firms can source the expertise needed to do all these things, as well as how best to choose and manage measurement vendors.

In chapter 9, we draw some conclusions about the state of the market and give pointers for the future. We end on a practical note with an appendix that provides answers to some frequently asked questions that we hear from HR and business leaders.

More than anything else, this book is a call to arms, a plea for action. Businesses themselves—not just outside vendors or expert consultants—need to act to make measurement work because only they can do so. If they do not, the current failure rates will remain as fixed for the next thirty years as they have been for the past thirty. And without progress in these rates, talent management as a whole will remain intrinsically limited in what it can achieve, and businesses will be missing an opportunity for better performance and shareholder value.

Companies may not have taken action yet, but the growing talent challenges and need for reliable talent intelligence provide

How to Read This Book

This book contains a lot of information, some of which is quite technical and some of which is very practical. We believe that having a basic understanding of technical issues is important for making good practical decisions about how to use talent measurement. So the earlier chapters of the book focus more on these technical issues, before we then move on to practical matters from about chapter 6 onward.

We hope that readers will go through the chapters in order. However, we are aware that different readers will be interested in different elements of the book, and that almost all readers will be very busy people. So:

- If you are mainly interested in reading an accessible summary of some of the latest technical research about how to measure talent, you could start with chapters 2 and 4.

- If you are more interested in understanding some of the practical considerations involved in choosing which measure, method, or tool to use, you could start with chapters 3 and 5 and the relevant sections in the appendix.

- If you are primarily interested in how best to implement and use talent measurement in your organization, you could begin with chapters 6, 7, and 8.

a compelling reason to do so now. Firms that do not act will not, of course, collapse overnight or notice a sudden drop in profits. Yet slowly and insidiously, their competitors who do act will gain ground on them. Big or small, global or local, organizations need to get this right. It is time to make measurement work.

2

STANDARD MEASURES OF TALENT

How Good Are They Really?

In 2011, close to 25 million people in the United Kingdom and United States alone tuned in to watch the *X-Factor* each week, a TV music competition in which aspiring singers compete for a recording contract. The winner is chosen by a celebrity panel and the audience at home, who phone in to vote for contestants. It is a franchise business, with versions screened in over forty countries: from *El Factor X* in Colombia to *XSeer Al Najah*, the pan-Arab version. Talent spotting has become entertainment for the masses, a casual evening activity, and we all think we can do it.

Dictionaries define X *factor* as a special quality or talent that is essential for success but difficult to describe. Yet over the past hundred years, this is precisely what psychologists have tried to do. They have tried to identify and describe the qualities essential for workplace success. Just like the *X-Factor* audience, most managers and leaders would probably claim to "know talent when they see it." What researchers have done is to check whether these ideas and hunches are correct, and in this chapter, we are going to look at what they have found.

It is a good place to start, because many businesses are unsure about what they should measure. So focusing on four main qualities that most assume are essential for success, we explore what the latest research can tell us about these factors. And in doing so, we will notice ways in which organizations currently often over- or underestimate the value of these standard measures of talent.

First, though, let's take a step back and consider how we can tell whether an ability or quality really is an X factor and reliable sign of talent.

Finding Dependable Measures of Talent

For some jobs, it is easy to test people's talent. If you are hiring a data entry clerk, for example, you could use a keystroke to evaluate his or her speed and accuracy entering data. With financial traders, you could simply look to see who makes the most money (assuming they have the same level of opportunity). Yet there are many jobs where measuring talent or results is not so easy and many situations, such as recruitment, where you do not have access to this information. So rather than measuring talent itself, we usually have to look for the signs and symptoms of it—particular behaviors or characteristics that we think are indicative of talent like intelligence, ambition, and conscientiousness.

For jobs where we are able to measure talent directly, creating measures of this talent tends to be fairly simple. All we need to do is to make sure that our measure accurately represents how good individuals are at this talent. But when we are measuring only the signs of talent, we need to make a second important check: whether the sign or factor we are measuring really is indicative of talent—so with intelligence, whether how bright someone is genuinely related to or predictive of workplace success. These two basic checks are important because they reveal whether a particular measure works and whether a specific factor really is a sign of talent. And as we look at some of the signs of talent that psychologists have tried to measure, we keep returning to these two questions.

For many years, it looked as if it would not be possible to find any signs or measures that reliably predict workplace success. Researchers found factors that appeared to predict performance in specific situations, yet when they looked at whether these factors could do so in different situations—in other jobs or companies—they usually found that they did not appear to be linked to success. Talent, it seemed, was a variable thing in that what was required to succeed in every job was different. There did not seem to be any single X factor.

In the 1970s, however, new statistical methods changed that belief. Researchers started using some sophisticated statistical methods to combine the results of multiple studies in a process known as meta-analysis. The difference this made was that instead of looking at single studies that used the results from, say, a hundred people, researchers were now able to combine the results from thousands of people. And when they did this, they found that some factors did appear to be common to success in a variety of jobs. They discovered that, yes, if you compared just two jobs or two companies, then what was required for success could be very different in each of them. But when you looked at all the jobs and companies together, certain things did seem to signal success in most situations.

We are going to look at four of the main potential indicators of talent that researchers have studied:

- *Prior experience*—what you have done before
- *Competencies and capabilities*—what you can do now
- *Intelligence*—how bright you are
- *Personality*—your personal characteristics, typical ways of behaving, and the attitudes you hold

Tens of thousands of research papers have been published on these four characteristics, but what follows will summarize the key findings for you in an accessible form. You may be surprised by some of this, as some of the factors that we often think of as important for talent do not in fact seem to be. At the same time, others are highly effective for companies wanting to get ahead of the game in spotting talent.

To begin, let's check what research has to say about most organizations' starting point in the hunt for talent: the experience that people bring.

Experience as a Sign of Talent

Typically the first thing we do is look at a résumé to see what individuals have done before. We look at what types of roles they have held, how long they have stayed in them, and what they have achieved. We look at their educational level, where they have lived and worked, and try to form a sense of what type of person they are. We do this because we assume that prior experience in roles similar to the one that we want them to fill now will enable them to perform better. And we do it because we assume that we can predict how well people will do in the future from how well they have done in the past. But can we?

Well, yes, but there are limits and challenges. Experience can clearly give people useful knowledge and skills that can help them succeed in a new role.[1] Sometimes that is all we really want to know: whether someone is sufficiently qualified and has the technical ability to do the job. In these cases, we can supplement a résumé with a test of technical knowledge or a work sample test in which we actually observe someone's skill at something. Studies have found that for highly technical or skilled jobs, these types of measures can be good at predicting performance.

Researchers have also found that prior experience can help us predict people's future performance in more general roles. Yet the results have not been as positive as we might expect.[2] The reason, it seems, is that there is more to experience than knowledge and skills. Every workplace has its own way of doing things, its own culture. It can leave people with habits, attitudes, and ways of working that may be well suited to one firm but do not fit a new job or company.[3] For instance, a common scenario is to meet a candidate for a senior role who has a strong background in terms of having already done similar jobs in other companies.

Yet he may previously have worked only in business cultures that are very different from the one of the company now considering employing him. So people's experiences can hinder or get in the way of their future performance just as they can help predict it.

The challenge this creates is that although the relevance of job knowledge and technical expertise is often obvious, the impact of experience on ways of working is typically less visible. As a result, we tend to overrate the value of experience by focusing more on the positives associated with it while overlooking the negatives.

Other factors also add to the difficulty of interpreting work experience. Over one-third of résumés are thought to contain inaccuracies, and people increasingly have less predictable career patterns.[4] In addition, the importance of various types of work experience can vary too. In many jobs, the experience of having carried out similar tasks before is more important for predicting success than whether a person has worked in a particular industry. But there are some roles (such as auditing) in which experience in a specific industry appears to be the more critical issue.[5]

Some of our most common assumptions about work experience are not supported by the evidence either. Here's one example that really surprised us. What would you think if you were comparing candidates and one of them had held five jobs in five years while the other had had only one job in that time? Most people will assume that the one-job person is the better candidate and that the five-job person is perhaps unreliable or unable to hold a job for long. Yet a recent study looking at over twenty thousand people found no relationship between how long people have lasted in previous jobs and how long they will stay in their next one.[6]

Biodata: A Somewhat More Systematic Attempt. Perhaps because of the difficulty in interpreting work experience, some companies have adopted a broader and more systematic approach to the issue. They collect information about a range of factors from the life histories of employees, referred to as biodata. They then analyze which experiences are most linked to outcomes like performance, retention, or avoiding accidents so that they can look for these things in job applicants. For example, one of the best predictors of training success among trainee pilots in World War II was purportedly the question, "Have you ever built and flown a model airplane"?[7]

What is important here is how broad a range of factors biodata can consider. Questions used can vary from the clearly work related ("How often were you late to work in your last job?") to the less obvious ("How many times did you have to take your driving test?"). They can even include the unbelievably odd ("How old were you when you first kissed someone romantically?").

The use of biodata has persisted because their ability to predict success is mainly good when the tools are well developed, with data collected from large numbers of people. (Small companies can still do this by acting in a consortium with other similar businesses.) And biodata seem to be able to predict a wide variety of things, from performance to absenteeism to ethical decision making.[8] Just how good a predictor these data are depends on the particular test used and what you are trying to predict. But validities of between 0.3 and 0.38 have been reported for predicting performance (see the box).[9]

Businesses, however, have not used biodata as much as we might expect given the good validities. Probably the main reason for this is that a lot of research on preferably thousands of employees is necessary to be able to identify which factors are the best predictors. This needs to be done individually too for each role and organization. In addition, no matter how useful they are, biodata factors sometimes just do not look right (psychologists would say that they lack *face validity*). In one study, for example, it turned out that the question that best predicted success in jewelry sales was, "How many times have you purchased real estate?" Furthermore, biodata do not help us understand why

Predictive Validity Explained

Throughout this book, to show how good particular measures are at predicting success, we refer to their *predictive validity*.

The validity figure is a number between 0 and 1 that indicates how strong the relationship is between a particular factor (such as experience) and a specific outcome (such as performance). If the validity is 0, this means that the factor is no better at predicting the outcome than chance. We might as well flip a coin. If the validity is 1, this means that the factor predicts the outcome perfectly every time; it is never wrong. In practice, a validity of 0.3 is considered good, and a validity of 0.5 is considered great. So when we say that biodata have a validity of somewhere between 0.3 and 0.38, that means the measure is pretty good at predicting performance.

Interestingly, the validity figure can also tell us what proportion or percentage of all the reasons people succeed is accounted for by the measure. To work this out, we simply square the validity number (multiply it by itself). A measure with a validity of 0.3 thus accounts for 9 percent of the reasons people succeed or not ($0.3 \times 0.3 = 0.9$, or 9 percent). And a validity figure of 0.38 for biodata means that it can account for up to 14 percent of the determinants of success. These figures do not sound large. Yet if we think about the sheer number of factors involved in determining people's behavior, they are fairly good.

For more detailed information on validity, including different ways of measuring it, see the section about it in the appendix.

factors like this predict something, which can limit both their usefulness and firms' level of comfort with using them.

Experience and Talent Overall. So we have found that having the right experience can indeed enable people to bring certain knowledge and skills that will help them perform well in a job. Yet it is not always obvious what the right experiences are, building good tools to measure them is not easy, and we tend to overlook the potential downsides of experience. Prior experience may be the first place we look for an indication of talent, but perhaps it should not be. Even when it is measured systematically, it is not the whole answer, and as we will see, it is not the best predictor. In our hunt for the X factor, we need to look elsewhere.

Competencies and Capabilities as Signs of Talent

Probably the second thing that most people look at when measuring talent is what is called competency or capability. Although some commentators have strong views about what is a competency and what a capability, the terms are widely used to refer to the same things. They are something of a catch-all phrase for knowledge, skills, abilities, and other characteristics (which you will sometimes see in research papers abbreviated as "KSAOs"). In other words, they refer to pretty much everything that is not experience. They are what people can do and how they tend to do it.

The idea of using competencies to spot talent gained popularity in the 1970s with the work of the noted American psychologist David McClelland.[10] He argued that we need to think about how competent people are not only in terms of their knowledge and skills, but also in terms of their broader behaviors, motives, and attitudes. Subsequent research has supported this idea too, showing, for example, that how leaders behave can affect both their individual and their company's results.[11]

When it comes to accurately measuring competencies, assessment centers (actually a process rather than a place, as we'll describe in chapter 4) are often cited as the most effective method. And there is evidence that competencies measured using assessment centers can predict performance with validities roughly on a par with collecting biodata—around 0.3 to 0.37.

This means that they can predict up to 14 percent of the causes of success.

However, assessment centers are not the most frequently used method of measuring competencies. More often the method is unstructured interviews, managers' ratings of their employees, or employees' self-ratings of their own capabilities. These may be easier and cheaper to implement than more formal measurement methods, but they also tend to be a lot less accurate. And for every drop in accuracy, the ability of competencies to predict performance is reduced.

Deciding Which Competencies to Measure. Perhaps the bigger challenge, though, is knowing which competencies to measure. There are, of course, some usual suspects that are commonly believed to be important no matter what the role—things like drive for results and decision-making and communication skills. Yet while these are largely accepted as necessary foundations for success, it is not clear that they are also what distinguishes great performers from ones who are just okay.

In theory, for each job family, a company would conduct an analysis of high and low performers to identify which competencies are the most essential. This level of detail is important because different roles require different competencies. A cosmetics salesperson in Germany, for example, requires a different set of competencies from a systems engineer in Indianapolis.

Merely in terms of the time and resources required, however, this kind of detailed job analysis is not practical in many organizations, so companies often cut corners. A common compromise is to apply the competencies that are identified in high performers in a particular role more broadly than is warranted. One national health care provider's competency framework, for instance, is applied to all leaders across all parts of the organization. This may sound fine, but the research on which it is based involved only a small group of senior executives.[12] Even assuming that their competencies are the right ones to take the business forward, it is not clear that what makes them successful is also required from all other leaders. Compromises like this may seem harmless, but as before, with each corner cut, the utility of competencies in predicting performance is reduced.

A common alternative is for companies to use generic competency frameworks developed by vendors. This is particularly common when trying to predict success a long way in advance—for example, when trying to predict which of a new group of graduates are most likely to be leaders of the future. These models can sound quite compelling. Vendors may be able to provide evidence that high performers in similar businesses tend to be strong in certain competencies. Yet this approach assumes that what has enabled others to succeed to date is the same as what will enable your business's people to succeed. And in many cases, this is just not so. Furthermore, since most of these frameworks are commoditized and owned by vendors, there is a lack of independent research into their efficacy.

Moreover, part of the challenge in trying to pinpoint which competencies are the most important for a particular job is that for most jobs, there is more than one way to do them well. This is especially so for more senior roles.[13] Researchers have found that the competencies that the best performers are rated highly on can vary even when these people are in very similar roles. In one study, for example, the competencies that top salespeople were rated highly on differed considerably.[14]

Implementation Challenges. So competencies are compelling and clearly potentially useful, but they also have implementation challenges that fundamentally undermine their usefulness. In the few instances where the link between competencies and performance is simple, clear, and close and a good measure exists, competencies can of course help identify talent. Yet beyond such instances, it is tough to find specific behaviors that can reliably predict performance. As noted above, competencies are often either not measured accurately or are not what is genuinely required for success. As with prior experience, using competencies to measure talent appears more popular than is justified by their actual efficacy.

   From Not So Good to Better. Already, then, we are beginning to see why selection failure rates have remained high for so long. The two main signs of talent that most businesses look at, experience and competencies, do not appear to be doing the job. This does not mean that they cannot, however. Indeed, there are some simple things that companies can do to improve the efficacy of these factors in predicting success. We look at these when we start exploring implementation issues in chapter 6. What is important for now, though, is that despite their common use, both have so far generally failed to fulfill their promise in helping identify talent.

   So what does work? Well, there are two main contenders left: intelligence and personality. Ironically, McClelland introduced the idea of competencies because he was disillusioned with the effectiveness of intelligence and personality tests. But as the years have passed, these measures have emerged as more promising options.

Intelligence as a Sign of Talent

Over the years, intelligence has been defined in many different ways and called many different things, most recently "reasoning ability" and "cognitive ability." Then there are the abbreviations: IQ (intelligence quotient), g (general intelligence), GCA (general cognitive ability), and GMA (general mental ability). Whatever we call it, the way we measure it has not changed in the hundred years since the first intelligence tests were devised.

   The French started it. In the late nineteenth century, the French government decided to identify children who needed specialized education programs and so ordered the creation of a test. By 1916 the test had been adapted for American populations, and for a while, intelligence tests were used mainly to predict academic performance. During World War I, though, military forces started using tests to screen people for service, and a large element of this tended to be intelligence testing.

In the 1960s, the use of intelligence tests took a knock as they became embroiled in political debates about racial differences in scores. But in the 1980s, new evidence emerged from meta-analyses that intelligence is indeed a reliable and capable predictor of work performance. Today it is widely regarded by many psychologists as the single best predictor of workplace success. It is not always the most important factor for every job in every circumstance, but overall, across all roles and all situations, it seems to be able to predict success better than any other factor. And given the growing complexity of the workplace, there is an argument to suggest that its importance is growing too. Just how good is it? A summary of over four hundred studies found that the validity of intelligence in predicting employees' performance was 0.38 for low-complexity jobs, roughly on a par with biodata. But for medium-complexity roles, the validity was 0.51, and for high-complexity jobs, it was as high as 0.57.[15] This would mean that for high-complexity jobs, it can account for over 32 percent of the causes of success. Given how unpredictable the world around us is, that really is incredible. Subsequent research has supported these findings and extended them to show that intelligence tests appear able to predict performance in almost all jobs in all cultures.

The Importance of Intelligence. There is more, though, for intelligence has also emerged as more important than any other personal characteristic in determining a whole host of different life outcomes.[16] The list is long but includes some highly relevant to the workplace:

- Educational achievement in elementary school, high school, and college

- Ultimate educational level attained
- Adult occupational level
- Adult income
- A wide variety of indexes of adjustment at all ages

In contrast, low scores on intelligence tests have been found to predict:

- Delinquency and criminal behavior
- Accident rates on the job
- Disciplinary problems in school
- Poverty
- Divorce
- Having an illegitimate child

Clearly some of these are politically laden findings and have stimulated often heated debate. What is important for our purpose is that intelligence has proved to be such a strong predictor of life and work success. This is why so many talent measurement processes use intelligence tests: they are perceived to be an efficient and effective means of identifying the brightest and best.

Asked how intelligence helps performance, most people suggest that it is by improving things like problem solving and decision making. And indeed some research has shown that intelligence levels are more important than experience for the ability to think strategically.[17] The biggest impact of intelligence, however, seems to be on the acquisition of job knowledge. Simply put, people higher in intelligence acquire more job knowledge and acquire it faster.[18] An excellent demonstration of the importance of this comes from a series of studies run by the US military in the 1980s. They found that recruits with below-average intelligence required more than three years to reach the same levels of performance than recruits with higher intelligence began with. Moreover, even with on-the-job experi-ence, enlistees with lower intelligence continue to lag behind those with higher intelligence.[19]

Limitations of Intelligence Tests. There are, of course, some limits to all this. For instance, intelligence does not seem to be equally good at predicting performance in all jobs. The research on this issue is not complete, but the ability of intelligence to predict sales performance, for example, has been found to be mixed.[20] In addition, there is some debate about the type of performance that intelligence can predict. Some researchers have found that it is better at predicting quantity and speed of work than quality of outputs.[21] Others have found that intelli-gence tends to predict best possible performance rather than typical day-to-day performance levels.[22]

In addition, intelligence levels may be so generally high in some environments that intelligence may not be an effective way of distinguishing between the good and the great.[23] We faced this difficulty recently when trying to use an intelligence test to evaluate applicants for roles in financial trading. The candidates were all so intelligent that the test could not discriminate among them.

There is also good anecdotal evidence that more intelligence is not always better. Beyond a certain level, individuals may "intellectualize" things too much and be insufficiently practical, which can have a negative impact on performance. This may be one of the reasons that low intelligence test scores have been shown to be better able to predict failure than high scores can predict success. It seems that while low intelligence may some-times be enough to ensure failure, high intelligence is not usually sufficient on its own to secure success, and too much of it can be counterproductive.

One last limitation with intelligence tests is that there is more to intelligence than is measured by many of these tests.[24]

For example, most people would agree that thinking styles and how we use our intelligence are important for success, yet these elements of intelligence have received surprisingly little attention by both researchers and vendors alike.[25]

There have, of course, been attempts to broaden how we measure intelligence and distinguish different types. For instance, in the 1980s, the psychologist Howard Gardner suggested that there are nine different types of intelligence that are all quite separate—things like linguistic, musical, and interpersonal intelligence. Yet subsequent research has shown that these abilities are all measured by standard intelligence tests and do not appear different at all. More promising is the concept of practical intelligence—the ability to deal with the problems and situations of everyday life.[26] It does not appear to be as strong a predictor of performance as standard intelligence tests, yet as a broader approach to thinking about intelligence, it does show merit.

Finally, there are measures of complexity of thought: the degree to which people are able to engage in strategic thinking. Some of these measures show promise, such as those based on Elliott Jaques's theory of categories of mental processes.[27] They are making substantial claims, too, with vendors reporting validities of over 0.7 or even 0.9. Nevertheless, caution is advised because of a lack of independent research into just how effective these measures are. What research does exist, then, is too limited to tell whether this approach can reliably produce these validities.

So the measurement of intelligence has its limits and needs to evolve further. It is the best predictor of talent available today for most types of jobs, especially more complex ones, but even at best estimates, it can account for only around 30 percent of the reasons behind performance. It may often be necessary for success, but on its own, it is not usually sufficient. Something else is involved.

Personality as a Sign of Talent

Character or personality is often claimed as the source of much success. In fact, most people seem intuitively to see it as more important than intelligence. In part, this is because there tends to be much more variability in personality than in levels of intelligence, and so it can appear more salient.[28] Yet for all its apparent importance, the emergence of personality tests for measuring talent is relatively new.

A Five-Factor Model. For many years, the use of personality tests in businesses was held back by the fact that they were mostly developed for clinical settings, and so did not feel or look right to organizations. And progress in developing new tests was hampered by the vast number of different models of personality used, which hindered researchers in comparing results and reaching conclusions. This all changed after World War II, though, with the development of tests designed for organizations and the emergence of a widely accepted model of personality: the five-factor model.

Not all tests available are based on the so-called Big Five factors this model describes. Yet it has been critical in enabling the industry to move forward because it has allowed researchers to compare findings and develop a shared body of knowledge. The model has changed over time, but its modern form has been around for twenty years. The five personality characteristics it describes are:

1. *Openness to experience.* The degree to which people like to learn new things, having a wide variety of interests, and being imaginative and insightful

2. *Conscientiousness.* The degree to which people like to be reliable, prompt, organized, methodical, and thorough

3. *Extraversion.* The degree to which people derive their energy from being with others and enjoy interacting with others

4. *Agreeableness*. The degree to which people are friendly, cooperative, and considerate

5. *Neuroticism or emotional stability*. The degree to which people are emotionally labile, experience negative emotions, and can seem moody or tense

From tests on thousands upon thousands of people, these five personality factors have been shown to be more or less distinct from one another. So generally, the score a person obtains on one of these dimensions will have little bearing on how he or she scores on the other four.

The model has generated a mass of research into the links between personality and performance. Overall, studies have found that of the five traits, neuroticism, extraversion, and conscientiousness are often the most relevant for job performance.[29] Unsurprisingly, different jobs appear to require different types of personality. Successful managers, for example, tend to be low in neuroticism and moderately high in extraversion and conscientiousness. For skilled and semiskilled jobs, conscientiousness and low neuroticism seem most important. For law enforcement jobs, low neuroticism, conscientiousness, and agreeableness all appear useful.[30] As a general rule, there seem to be no jobs in which being high in neuroticism or low in conscientiousness is desirable.

Of all the five factors, conscientiousness has generated the most enthusiasm. In fact, one recent study showed that HR professionals believe it to be more predictive of performance than intelligence.[31] In reality, though, the validity of conscientiousness is usually estimated to be between 0.22 and 0.28, below that of intelligence tests.[32] Indeed, these validities mean that on its own, conscientiousness can account for only between 5 and 8 percent of the reasons for success.

The link between conscientiousness and performance is not straightforward either. It appears, for example, to be more important for some jobs than others, and possibly less important for managers than other staff.[33] It also seems to be a better predictor of performance in experienced employees than in new employees or applicants.[34] Finally, high levels of conscientiousness may actually be a negative sign for success in some roles because it can lead to behavior that is seen as bureaucratic and indecisive.[35]

One of the difficulties for businesses in using personality tools is that interpreting what results mean and which characteristics are most important for which roles is not easy. Interestingly, the research has not confirmed most people's intuitive beliefs about the relative importance of character. Of all the studies done, hardly any have found validities for personality traits to predict performance above the level of 0.30.[36] This means that personality tests do not appear able to account for more than 9 percent of the reasons that people succeed or fail. Moreover, even these validities may be overestimated, since evidence has recently been found that publication bias—the tendency to publish only positive results—may have inflated results.[37]

Beyond the Five Factors. So why do we all think that character is important for success, but the research does not back us up? Just as with competencies, one of the problems is likely to be that no single type of personality is the key to success. There is also the issue of how effectively we are measuring personality. One increasingly recurring theme here is that progress may have been limited by the five-factor model that has enabled the industry to get this far. Although the model has been useful in allowing researchers to progress in their work, test developers may need to look beyond it to develop better tools.

For example, each of the five factors is made up of additional, more specific characteristics. Although these components are described differently by different researchers, it has been suggested, for example, that conscientiousness consists of hard work, orderliness, conformity, and dependability.[38] What is interesting is that studies have shown that these more specific components of the five factors may be more able to predict success than the Big Five.[39]

This may sound odd. If conscientiousness is made up of dependability and orderliness, how can these individual components be better predictors of success than conscientiousness itself? Well, to give an example, writing a book arguably has a lot to do with orderliness but is a lot less about dependability and conformity. If we measure these things separately, we may thus find that orderliness is a good predictor of book-writing success but that dependability and conformity are less effective. So when we bundle all these elements into a single thing—conscientiousness—we combine good predictors with less effective ones. As a result, conscientiousness as a whole ends up being less effective than the best of its more specific ingredients.

The five-factor model has also been criticized for not being complete or sufficiently business focused. Some alternative models and approaches have been suggested, and a new generation of tests is emerging.[40] None of these has yet challenged the Big Five's dominance in research circles, but two types show particular promise in helping businesses spot talent.

First, a number of tools with more business-focused language are being developed. Saville Consulting's Wave test, for one, certainly sounds very different from traditional personality tests, with factors such as "Adapting Approaches" and "Influencing People." It may be doing something different too, since a comparison study with traditional personality tests has suggested that it can exceed them for validity, with levels over 0.45.[41] Caution is required since more independent research is needed to confirm these findings. Yet the approach of developing more business-oriented tools clearly has promise for organizations.

Second, there is the idea of personality derailers. This work turns on its head the traditional assumption that lack of success is due to people not having the "right stuff." It suggests instead that people who do not succeed may have some "wrong stuff," or unhelpful personal characteristics.[42] Derailers could be considered competencies, but many of the measurement tools available are based on personality characteristics. The idea has been popularized by Sydney Finkelstein's book, *Why Smart Executives Fail*, and by the Hogan "Dark Side" personality tests, which try to measure potential derailing behaviors.[43] Judging by the popularity of these tests, the idea seems to be striking a chord with many businesses. Again, though, caution is necessary. Although there is some evidence that these measures may predict things like staff turnover, in general the validity evidence for them is scarce at present. As with intelligence tests, choosing the right personality measure for your needs can be challenging, a topic we come back to in chapter 5.

What is clear is that personality tests do not currently appear to be as useful in our hunt for the X factor as we might expect. We say *currently* because, like many other people, we believe that character *is* important for success. And we are convinced that with time, better tests will be produced that are capable of showing how character helps. In fact, we come back to one very important role that personality tests can play in the next chapter. The challenge right now, though, is that most personality tests do not do as good a job as we would hope in helping to predict performance. Personality might indeed be more important for success than intelligence. But for the moment, talent measures are not able to prove this and show how.

Values, Social Skills, and Other Possible Signs of Talent

Experience, competencies, intelligence, and personality are, then, the four main places that we have tended to hunt talent. Several others are worth mentioning, though. For example, measuring values and integrity, although not new, has become an increasingly popular avenue for research over the past ten years. For the most part, the purpose of these measures is to help detect people who may engage in what are called counterproductive work behaviors—everything from stealing to being prone to accidents. And these tools have generally proved effective at doing this (we look at this is more detail in the appendix).

Yet these tools have also been used to try to predict success. Alignment between the values of managers and their business has been shown to be related to both individuals' success and their intention to remain with a firm.[44] And some integrity tests that are based on Big Five personality measures appear able to predict overall performance levels at validity levels roughly on a par with the best personality tests.[45]

Measuring values more generally can be problematic, however. There are suggestions that tests of values are too easy to fake and are thus unreliable as a source of information. And it sometimes seems that the move to measure values appears driven more by idealism than by the potential efficacy of values as a predictor of success. A major oil multinational recently discovered this when it replaced its competency model with a values framework that described six core values of the business. Yet it soon found that the information gained from rating the six values was not enough to make selection decisions and so had to reintroduce a competency model alongside the values.

Testing social and political skills is another option. These tests have become increasingly popular as companies have become larger and more global—and more reliant on such skills. Research has shown that these measures pick up something different from intelligence and personality tests and that they may indeed be able to help predict managerial performance.[46] Yet the best way to measure these skills is still not clear. For a while, many people advocated tests of emotional intelligence, but recent studies have shown that these measures have disappointing validity levels.[47] More recently, measures of social capital have appeared that look at the size and shape of individuals' social networks. These tools certainly look interesting and are getting some headlines, but as yet remain unproven in their ability to predict success.

One other area of study is motivation and drive. The desire to achieve objectives has, hardly surprisingly, been shown to predict performance.[48] Yet tests of motivation are relatively rare, and the findings of the research that does exist are mixed when it comes to the importance of different types of motivation for performance.

So as with the main four factors studied, there is promise and some progress in each of these other possible signs of talent but no clear way forward—yet.

Finding a Way Forward

What, then, are the signs of success that businesses should use to identify talent? In this chapter, we have looked at the main factors commonly measured and have reviewed evidence about the ability of each to predict success. We have discovered that all have some predictive validity, which means that all are better than mere chance at predicting success. So to some extent, we are right to look at these factors because they all have the potential to help us spot talent and make decisions about people in some situations.

Yet we have also seen that generally these standard markers of talent have limitations and implementation issues that make them less effective as measures than we might expect. No single, special X factor seems to exist, and we need to be careful in attributing too much to the results of any one measure.

Intelligence may be as close as we will ever get to finding such a factor. And given the number of variables involved in determining success, the fact that intelligence alone can account for up to 30 percent of the reasons that people succeed in some types of roles is genuinely impressive. But intelligence is not equally important for all roles and so has its limits. There simply is no one thing that is the key to predicting success in all situations, no magic bullet to measure that we can always use to spot talent.

This is probably not surprising. After all, most people would agree that success is not just about having one quality in abundance. Instead, it is typically about having the right combination of qualities. But how then can businesses determine which combinations of measures are the best to use? And is there anything they can do to boost their chances of spotting talent and accurately predicting success? It is these critical questions that we address in the next chapter.

3

RETHINKING MEASUREMENT

How Best to Predict Success

If the discussion forums on networking sites like LinkedIn are anything to go by, many businesses find choosing which signs of talent to measure confusing. The forums teem with requests for suggestions of which measures to use, and the answers provided often do not seem to make things any clearer. That there is some confusion is not surprising. As we saw in the previous chapter, there is no one sign of talent that you should always measure, and the ability of most measures to predict success remains frustratingly low. Yet as we will show in this chapter, there are some clear guidelines that all businesses can follow that make the task of knowing what to measure easier and can fundamentally improve firms' ability to spot talent and predict success.

We begin by presenting some guiding principles for deciding what to measure and choosing which combinations of factors will enable you to best predict success. We then take a brief detour to check whether these guiding principles also apply to something that is often seen as very different to measuring someone's ability to do a job: measuring his or her long-term potential. Finally, we look at what businesses can do to boost their ability to predict success, no matter what measures they use. The solution, as we will see, promises to fundamentally change both how we think about measurement and our ability to accurately identify and measure talent.

Three Principles for Deciding What to Measure

As we saw in the previous chapter, a basic challenge with talent measurement is deciding what to measure. In our experience, three guiding principles can help organizations determine which measures to use:

- Measure what you need.
- Ask about validity.
- Ask about incremental validity.

Measure What You Need

The way companies typically approach deciding what to measure is through analyzing the skills and qualities that specific roles, teams, or business units need. This involves defining role requirements or what the company needs people to do. Sometimes this is achieved through a formal process like a job analysis, and in some countries having a structured job description is actually a legal requirement. Other times and in other countries, requirements are defined through more informal or intuitive means. Yet it is always there to some degree, even if it is just an idea in the hiring manager's mind. There is a picture or list, then, of what you need and are looking for.

What is important is to make sure that this list is explicitly stated and clearly distinguishes the two or three things that are most critical for ensuring that people succeed. Then, wherever possible, ensure that your choice of measures is led by this list of most critical qualities or competencies by the type of talent the business needs. As principles go, it may sound obvious, but it is too often overlooked.

Ask About Validity

Sometimes, of course, there is only a vague idea of what a role or the business needs, and other times the list of what is required is just too long. When this happens and there are thus no clear requirements for guiding the decision of what to measure, businesses tend to revert to what they know or feel familiar with. This is a bad idea.

As we have seen, there is no one measure that you should always use: different jobs require different qualities. So if you always use the same set of measures and tests for all roles, the chances are that sometimes they will not help you much, and they may even be misleading.

Instead of reverting to the familiar, then, when choosing what to measure, the one question all businesses should always ask is this: "How predictive of success is this factor in this particular type of role?" or, in other words, "How valid is this measure?" Because validity figures can tell you whether a measure predicts performance, checking validity is a way of checking that you are genuinely measuring what you need.

We have encountered many leaders who do not seem to be in the slightest bit interested in validity, which we frankly find amazing. If you are going to pay good money for measurement results, then you need to make sure that the information they are providing is accurate and relevant. On a purely commercial level, anything else is just bad business.

Validity is a technical subject and can be complicated. So in chapter 5, we present a list of specific questions that you can ask about the validity of measures to help you decide whether they can help you predict success. For the moment, though, we just want to highlight the basic rule that you should always ask about validity. In other words, be led by the facts and science, not by traditions or familiarity.

Ask About Incremental Validity

Asking about validity can help you understand which measures are the most predictive of success. Yet as we have noted, talent is made up of a mix of multiple qualities and abilities, so you need to use multiple measures, and to work out which combination is best, you need to ask a different question. Just asking about validities will not work. This is because when you ask how valid a particular test is, you are asking how good a measure it is on its own, separate from anything else.

To work out what the best combination is requires a different question: one about incremental validity. This is the amount of validity that one measure has over and above another one: how much additional information or validity it provides with whatever other measures you are using. For example, we know that personality-based integrity tests are nowhere near as good as intelligence measures when it comes to predicting success. On this basis, we might decide not to use them. But when we look at the incremental validity they offer over intelligence tests, it is a very different story. We find that they can add around 0.14 validity points to the 0.5 or so validity figure that intelligence measures give us.[1] So we now have total validities of 0.64, which are able to account for over 40 percent of the causes of success. Likewise, personality tests appear to offer some decent incremental validity over intelligence with most roles, though precisely how much depends on the role and the tests used.[2]

Sometimes, of course, measures that you might expect to offer incremental validity do not. There is evidence, for instance, that if you already use both intelligence and personality tests, adding a measure of emotional intelligence will offer little extra validity.[3] Another example comes from the combination of intelligence tests with work sample tests. For medium-complexity jobs, the validity of intelligence tests is about 0.51, and for work sample tests, it is around 0.54. On this basis, you might think that by combining the two, you would get a superb predictor of success. Unfortunately, this is not the case.

Research shows that performance on work sample tests is largely a consequence of intelligence: intelligent people tend to do better on them. In other words, a large part of what work sample tests measure is intelligence. As a result, they offer little incremental validity over intelligence tests.[4] It might look as if they are measuring different things, but by asking about incremental validity, you can see that they are assessing more or less the same thing.

Incremental validity is thus the reason that using more measures is not always better. We recently met representatives of one company that used seven different psychometric tests in its recruitment processes in addition to interviews. They simply assumed that the more tests they had, the more able they would be to predict performance. Yet had they considered the incremental validity that each offered over the others, they would have found that this is not the case.

So while it might be tempting to use as many as possible of whichever tests have the highest validities, focusing only on validity is likely to lead to the wrong combinations or at least not the best ones. Asking about incremental validity can make all the difference: it is the yardstick for gauging which combinations of factors are the most predictive of success.

Since different jobs require different qualities, the most effective combination will vary between roles and companies. Yet as a general guide, we recommend you begin by identifying a foundation for your measurement process, such as a specific competency or job criterion. This is typically the most important thing that the business in general or a role in particular needs from the individuals being measured. You can then look to see which among the measures that you could use and are relevant to the role offer you the best incremental validity over your starting point.

And the next time a vendor shows you a measure, do not be satisfied just with knowing what its validity is. Ask what level of incremental validity it can offer over the other factors you are measuring. Because little research has been conducted on this issue so far, chances are that they may not know the answer for the specific tests you are considering. Nevertheless, they should have a general idea, and asking the question will focus both you and them on the issue and thereby help ensure that you get effective combinations of measures and do not employ redundant tests.

Measuring Potential

Focusing on these three basic principles will help you choose which factors to measure in most situations, but there is one specific scenario that is often viewed as a very different type of measurement: the increasingly common tendency for businesses to measure individuals' long-term potential to succeed. The goal in doing so is to identify the people who are most likely to be promoted or could be top performers or future leaders in three, five, or even ten years.[5] As if spotting talent and predicting success in the short term were not difficult enough, it seems we sometimes need to do it through a long lens.

The issue here is that it is commonly believed that the qualities required to succeed in the long term are different from what it takes to succeed in the short term. As a result, businesses commonly measure one set of factors to gauge someone's talent for a particular role and a different set of factors to evaluate his or her long-term potential.

These factors for assessing potential are often referred to as a *potential model*, and because almost every measurement vendor has its own such model, an almost endless number of them are available. In the United Kingdom, for example, one model frequently used includes the factors of drive, intellect, and influencing ability. A second model, more common in the United States, is that of ability, ambition, and attitudes. And a third approach is the idea that the best predictor of long-term success is the ability to learn.

Judging by the popularity of these models, businesses appear to have a lot of faith in them. They seem to make sense and to be intuitively compelling. A person who has high levels of drive, intellect, influence, and learning ability certainly sounds like someone who would be successful. There is research to support the use of some of these characteristics too. Intellect, of course, involves intelligence, which is seen by many as the single best predictor available. Learning ability, meanwhile, appears to be predictive of current performance levels and the likelihood of promotion in the short term.[6] And although ambition has been studied surprisingly little, there is some evidence that it may predict success, and possibly better than any of the Big Five personality factors.[7]

The Problem with Potential

All of this sounds good, and many of the potential models used are touted as being highly able to predict success. Some vendors even suggest they can do this many years in advance with validity levels exceeding 0.70. This would mean that they can account for around 50 percent of the reasons people succeed or not. However, few of the models and tools that abound have been independently validated, and there is a general lack of evidence about which factors can best predict long-term success. From the research that has been done, though, two broad conclusions can be drawn about which factors to measure when gauging long-term potential.

First, the factors that are most able to predict long-term success are generally the same as those that best predict current performance. If you look at some specific roles, this might not be true. The factors that predict current performance in information technology engineers, for example, may be slightly different from those that predict which engineers will reach the top of the profession. Technical expertise, for one, may be more important for current performance. But if you look overall at the general indicators of long-term potential across all roles, they are pretty similar to what predicts short-term performance.

Second, there is no conclusive evidence that long-term success can be predicted with much accuracy by any model or single pattern of characteristics. Looking at particular combinations of personal qualities can, of course, be better than merely relying on random chance to identify those with high potential. But let's not kid ourselves. Given the sheer number of variables involved in determining success over long periods of time, identifying potential is very difficult. From a purely technical viewpoint, trying to accurately predict potential is like trying to shoot an ant from a mile away. At night.

How to Predict Long-Term Success

So what should you do if you need to try to measure potential? After all, many businesses rely on these ratings to guide developmental investment. In general, the three principles we have described for choosing what to measure apply just as much to when you are trying to measure long-term potential as to when you are trying to predict short-term success. You must ask what type of talent the business needs. Which of these abilities and qualities are most able to predict success? And which combinations of factors give the highest validities? To help decide how to measure potential, though, there are a few extra guidelines we would add:

○ *Do not feel that you need to use a specialist measure of potential.* By all means, supplement your evaluations of performance with other measures, but they do not need to be specialist models of potential. Remember: depending on the role, a combination of intelligence and personality tests can predict success with a total validity of between 0.55 and 0.65. A specialist measure of potential will need to match or better this.

○ *Do not look too far ahead.* The further ahead you try to predict success, the less likely it is that you will be right. To have a decent chance of accurately predicting which people are most likely to be successful, focus on just trying to identify who has the potential to be promoted to the next level. This will make it easier to define what abilities and qualities are most required to succeed and improve your chances of being right.

○ *Use more than one model of potential across the business.* The factors that are required for success are likely to vary at different levels of the business. For example, the characteristics that most accurately identify potential for advancement in executives will probably be different from those that predict potential in graduates. They may also vary in different functions or parts of the business.

○ *Answer the question, "Potential for what?"* No one has potential that he or she will fulfill no matter what. We all need certain circumstances or environments in order to fulfill our potential. A polar bear may be an extraordinary animal, but it is not going to do well on a hot beach. Many readers probably know of people who have been successful in one job, only to fail in another. A common example of this is turnaround leaders. They typically have the drive and edge to pull a business back from the brink. Yet they may struggle once things have been turned around if they do not also possess the more nurturing qualities required to build and develop.

Wherever possible, then, make sure that measures do not just say how much potential someone has but also what he or she has potential for—that is, the types of roles and work environments individuals are most likely to succeed in. For managers who are simply rating potential as part of an annual appraisal, this may be an unnecessary complication. But for more formal methods and tools, it should be a requirement.

This latter point may surprise some readers. After all, it is commonplace now for businesses to rate people's general overall potential. Yet it is a critical point and touches on an issue that lurks behind all measurement: the importance of context. The fact is that whether someone succeeds is determined not just by how talented he or she is but also by things like the opportunities this person has and the business environment he or she is operating in. And as we will now go on to see, it is in this all-too-often-overlooked issue that we can find an important clue to how we can fundamentally change and improve our ability to predict success.

From Talent Measurement to Talent Matching

If you look across the measurement market, there are plenty of vendors saying that they have new and radically improved measures, advertising them with claims that "assessment will never be the same again." A great illustration of this is the recent trend among some vendors to compete over the size of their benchmarks, that is, the number of people they have tested. The idea is that the more people they have measured, the better able they are to know industry standards. Yet for all their uses, bigger benchmarks are not genuine game changers. Instead, the reality is that overall, measures are no more predictive today than they were thirty years ago. Developments have yielded newer measures, shorter ones, and smarter ones, but they have not produced substantially more predictive ones.[8]

Some progress will undoubtedly come from developing current measures. We have seen, for example, the move toward broader measures of intelligence and more specific measures of personality. Yet to substantially improve our ability to predict success, we are going to need to start doing something fundamentally different.

The solution, as we have hinted, lies in the interaction between individuals' talents and the needs and demands of their environment. This is something that is actually already taken into account in selection processes, in that there is typically a job description against which individuals' abilities can be assessed. So we already assume that whether people will succeed is a function not only of the qualities they possess but also of the level of fit between them and the job.

The Importance of Fit

The importance of the level of fit between people's talents and the demands of their jobs can be seen in a study that looked at the impact of General Electric (GE) leaders when they moved to new companies.[9] GE is a particularly interesting example, since it deliberately tried to develop leaders with a range of experiences who would possess generic leadership skills that they could transport into any role. They were the personification of the "martini" manager, who would be good "anytime, anyplace, anywhere." The market certainly seemed to believe this, anyway. In 85 percent of cases, the hiring company's stock price rose as soon as it was announced that a CEO from GE had been appointed.

The researchers, however, wanted to check if this faith was warranted, so they categorized both the strategic challenges facing each company and, using résumés, the skill sets of the former GE leaders (distinguishing between different types of leadership experiences). They then divided the CEOs into two groups. In one there was a good match between business need and the leaders' skill sets, and in the other there was a mismatch. They found that the performance of the businesses where there was a good match with the leader's skills was over double that of the mismatched group. So leadership skills do not appear to be as transportable as has sometimes been thought, and ensuring good person-job fit pays. Literally.

The vast majority of companies realize this. There may have been a time when picking the best people was all that mattered. These days, though, we generally try to pick the best people for a particular job. We have job descriptions to match people's skills against. Even when we are assessing people for developmental purposes, we usually evaluate them with an eye to how effective they will be in their roles. The problem, however, is that our judgments about fit at present suffer from two big flaws: they are too implicit and too narrow. Let's briefly look at each of these.

The Need to Make Fit More Explicit. Although recruiters usually consider how well someone will be able to do a job, rarely do we see an actual rating of fit. This may not seem significant, but it is. Without such a rating, it is not clear to what degree managers are focusing on this in their selection decisions. So the first step to take in improving our ability to predict success is to ensure, wherever possible, that an actual score is given for the level of fit between a person and a role. We have to shift the emphasis in talent measurement away from who is the best to who is the best fit—in other words, away from talent measurement and toward talent matching.

The importance of this can be seen in the risks associated with using "leadership index" ratings. These are single, overall scores of how good a leader someone is in general—effectively, of how good a "martini leader" she is. These ratings have obvious appeal in that they are clear and simple, but the evidence shows that they are too simplistic because few people—if any—are equally good in all situations. A single rating of how good a leader someone is overall may seem attractive, but it is a mirage and dooms us to being able to predict success with only limited accuracy. People are not simply good. They are good at something and in certain circumstances. So if we are to turn talent data into proper talent intelligence, we need to understand the issue of fit and explicitly measure it.

The Need to Broaden Fit. Even when we are presumably measuring fit, we tend to do so in too narrow a way. There is little doubt that people's performance is affected by the environment they work in—things like their relationship with their boss, the colleagues they work with, and the business culture. Yet we typically do not explicitly measure the level of fit between individuals and these environmental factors.

The importance of this is that broader factors have repeatedly been shown to be critical to success. In the 1970s, for example, a study at Exxon looked at the impact of four environmental factors on managerial success:

- Challenge of first job assignment
- Life stability
- Personality match between manager and his or her report
- Immediate manager's success

The researchers found that these factors accounted for as much as 22 percent of the factors determining performance in addition to what was already predicted by intelligence and personality.[10]

More recently, a study asked managers how satisfied they were with the quality of new contract employees.[11] Splitting the managers into three groups, based on whether they thought the quality of contract talent was high, medium, or low, the researchers looked at what was different about the hiring practices. They discovered that considering cultural fit appeared to be more important for securing high-quality talent than was having detailed job descriptions.

Environment is not just critical to performance, though. It can also affect the ability of some of the more standard signs of talent to predict success. For example, in business cultures where people have a high degree of autonomy, personality appears to be a more important factor for success than in settings with low autonomy.[12] And conscientiousness may be more important for success in environments where there are high levels of organizational politics.[13]

Likewise, intelligence seems to be a better predictor of leadership effectiveness in low-stress situations and for tasks that require higher levels of direction.[14] And the relationship between the intelligence of leaders and that of their teams appears critical. If there is too big a difference between them, superior intelligence can even be detrimental to a leader's chances of success.[15] In short, if we do not start looking at the environment in which performance takes place, we will struggle to make sense of why some people fail despite showing great promise and why others succeed despite all evidence to the contrary.

Businesses have not completely ignored the broader environment, of course. For a few decades, measuring cultural fit has regularly been part of the selection process for overseas assignments, but it has not really spread beyond this narrow application. One increasingly common practice is for organizations to try to identify and select individuals who fit their company values and norms. However, like competency models, values frameworks are often aspirational rather than reflective. Measuring people's values has technical challenges, too, since they are said to be too easy to fake and so unreliable as a source of information.

So which aspects of the way people match their environment should we be measuring?

Four Useful Types of Fit

Matching people with roles usually involves four different types of fit (see figure 3.1):

- *Person-job fit:* The degree of fit between a person's qualities and the requirements of a particular role
- *Person-organization fit:* The degree of fit between a person's characteristics and the working environment or culture
- *Person-team fit:* The degree of fit between a person and the colleagues he or she will be working most closely with
- *Person-manager fit:* The degree of fit between a person and the manager she or he will be working for

Figure 3.1 Measuring Fit

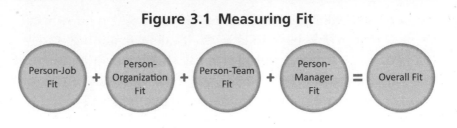

A review of 172 studies found that these four types of fit were more or less distinct. It also found that they all matter.[16] As we would expect, person-job fit is important for predicting performance, productivity, job satisfaction, and reduced job stress.[17] Person-organization fit, by contrast, seems to be the best predictor of commitment, organizational citizenship behaviors, and staff turnover.[18] Person-team fit has been less studied but appears to predict the quality of relationships with coworkers. And finally, person-manager fit predicts both employees' satisfaction levels with their manager and turnover.[19] As the old adage says, people join companies but leave bosses.

It is worth pointing out that when we say "fit," we do not necessarily mean "similarity." For example, there is some suggestion that performance levels may be greater when managers and employees have different personality traits.[20] Likewise, diversity among team members may be a liability or an asset depending on the type of role.[21] Where innovation or experimentation is important, diversity is likely to enhance performance. Yet for tasks focusing on production or execution, homogeneous teams may outperform diverse ones.[22]

Three Steps for Measuring Fit

So what does this mean for how we approach talent measurement and for how we can turn talent data into talent intelligence? We have three key recommendations:

1. Environmental/contextual factors should be added to job descriptions and included in key selection criteria—this is

because before you can measure fit, you need to know what it is that people have to fit with. If talent matching is to become an integral part of the way that companies do measurement, it needs to become a standard element of job descriptions. We return to this in chapter 6 when we look at implementing talent measurement.

2. When reviewing individuals' record of past success through interviews or résumés, make sure that the transferability of this success is considered. Ensure, then, that managers and recruiters focus not only on what people have achieved and how, but also on the environment in which they achieved it.[23]

3. In addition to person-job fit, organizations should explicitly measure person-organization, person-team, and person-manager fit in all selection and developmental talent measurement processes.

These suggestions may sound more daunting than they really are. Managers usually already make implicit decisions about each of these things.[24] What we are suggesting is making these judgments more explicit, visible, and informed. And we should be more explicit because being implicit is not working. A study of more than twenty-eight thousand newly hired employees found that businesses get the right person for the job on the majority of occasions but that they get the right person for the organization only 29 percent of the time.

This does not need to be complex. For example, as an easy minimum, organizations could require assessors and decision-making managers to provide a simple rating of each of these four types of fit. The fit ratings can then be added to give an overall score, or they can be weighted differently to emphasize particular types of fit.

Of course, it is possible to go further. Personality and cultural tests already exist that make it possible to compare individuals' personalities with the prevailing organizational culture or with a manager's own personality and ways of working. The globally used PAPI personality test, for example, comes with a job-profiler tool, which allows managers or job experts to complete a short questionnaire that determines the requirements of the role. The final test report is thus able not just to describe an individual's personality but also to show how this may or may not fit with the requirements of the role.

Indeed, the issue of fit seems to be where personality and character factors finally demonstrate the levels of importance in predicting success that we would expect them to. We showed in the previous chapter that personality tests have largely been disappointingly poor at predicting performance, at least compared to intelligence tests. But for measuring person-organization fit, person-team fit, and person-manager fit, personality is likely to be our best bet.

Moreover, there is some evidence that developing specific personality measures for a particular business may be more effective than using off-the-shelf generic personality measures.[25] Since this is not often currently done, there needs to be more research into the matter, and obviously it would make sense only for larger organizations. But as a longer-term option, it could be worth exploring.

Not every firm can or needs to go this far, though. The three core steps for using fit we have proposed are very simple, even simplistic. Yet they have the potential to fundamentally change how we think about measurement and significantly improve our ability to measure talent and thus also our people decisions.

The opportunity here lies in what we have traditionally used talent measurement for. When we are told that someone is a good performer, the most common response is usually, "Compared to whom?" or "At what?" And in general, the talent measurement market to date has been more focused on answering the first question than the second. It has largely concentrated, then, on trying to identify the brightest person, the most driven, and the best—hence, the current popularity of generic bench-marks that help businesses understand how good their people are compared to those in other firms.

Benchmarks can certainly be interesting and useful, but they have limits. Because by not more explicitly focusing on fit and sufficiently considering context, they leave out a large part of the picture. To develop real talent intelligence, achieve value-adding talent insight, and genuinely make some meaningful business impact with talent measurement, we need to be able to answer the, "At what?" question. The good news is that we can, and the key to doing so is the issue of fit.

Changing Talent Measurement

In the previous chapter, we looked at some of the factors that businesses have commonly tried to measure in order to identify talent and predict success. We discovered that many of these measures are less effective than we might have imagined and that no single, special X factor seems to exist.

In this chapter, we have looked at what businesses can do to make the most of these measures and improve their ability to measure talent accurately. We have looked at how following three principles can make choosing the right measures simpler for measuring both immediate talent and long-term potential. We have emphasized the importance of being clear about what the business and particular roles need and the criticality of check-ing the predictive validity of the factors you intend to measure.

We have also looked at how to select combinations of mea-sures by considering incremental validity and at how choosing what to measure when trying to identify long-term potential need not be very different from choosing how to measure short-term success. Finally, we explored how firms can improve their ability to predict success by more explicitly and broadly consid-ering fit and suggested three ways in which this can be implemented.

Rather than looking to the market for solutions, organizations must start leading the way. If firms start focusing on these issues, the measurement market will follow and start producing more sophisticated measures to help them. And if enough businesses make the changes, we stand to achieve nothing less than a transformation and reenergizing of the talent measurement arena.

In chapters 2 and 3, we have focused on what to measure, describing the most common signs of success that are measured, their utility, their limitations, and how to improve them. Now, in the next two chapters, we look at how to measure them: at the various methods, tools, and techniques that are available and how best to choose which to use.

4

TOOLS OF THE TRADE

Eight Processes for Gathering Data

Knowing what you are looking for is one thing; working out how best to see it is another. For this, you need the tools of the trade: the measurement methods, tests, and instruments that enable you to assess both the standard signs of talent, such as intelligence and personality, and the different types of fit. You will already be familiar with many of these tools. Yet just as with what to measure, there are some common misperceptions about how to measure and which tools are best to use.

In this chapter, we look at eight major measurement methods, from everyday methods, such as interviews, to deeply technical ones, such as psychometrics and situational judgment tests. For each method, we review the latest research, reveal key points, and explore what it can and cannot do. In chapter 5, we then consider some guidelines for how to decide which method or methods to use.

First, though, we address a more basic question: Why do we need formal measurement methods at all? Why not just ask candidates and those who know them what their talents are, and let things go at that? The answer, which comes down to problems of bias, may seem obvious. But considering it more closely can help us to understand the fundamental challenges facing all measurement methods and thus guide decisions about which tools to use.

Two Basic Ways of Measuring Talent

If you want to know how talented someone is at something, in theory your two best options are testing performance or measuring his or her actual results. Yet in today's work environment, there are few aspects of performance that you can test directly without asking someone's opinion, especially in complex roles. And as we described in chapter 2, measuring results is often not straightforward. It can be hard to know whether outcomes are due to genuine talent or other factors like opportunity or plain luck.

This leaves you two options: ask people themselves how good they are or ask someone else (like their manager). In fact these are the two most common ways of obtaining information about people's talent, and most measurement methods involve at least one of them.

Asking People Themselves

So can people accurately rate how good they are at something? The consensus from research is that most people do have a reasonable sense of whether they have some skill in something. For example, they know whether they can drive a truck and if they are closer to being a novice or an expert. What they are less able to do is to make specific, accurate ratings of how good they are compared to others.

For instance, if you look at everyone overall, you find that people tend to slightly overrate their abilities.[1] This is particularly true when they believe that the rating will have some consequence for them, as when it is used in appraisals or to inform selection decisions. Yet this general tendency hides some big individual differences. People vary significantly in the degree to which they over- or underrate themselves.[2] Some people overrate greatly, and others underrate, so a big problem with self-ratings is their reliability: that their accuracy can vary greatly from one person to the next. And adding spice to this is the

Dunning-Kruger effect: the finding that people of low ability tend to overrate themselves, while people of high ability tend to underrate themselves.[3]

These tendencies to over- or underrate are examples of what are formally called *ratings bias*, *judgment errors*, or *response distortion*. They are the enemy of accurate measurement, and almost every evaluation you make is affected by them to some degree. Some people, for instance, always tend to respond positively to "yes or no" and "true or false" questions.[4] Others tend to respond either more moderately or more extremely. Women, for example, tend to give more extreme ratings than men do.[5] And research has shown that demographic and geographical cultural differences can affect how people rate themselves too.[6] Just think of the stereotypical British way of describing something they like as "not bad" versus the American "great."

Together these issues make it difficult to obtain an accurate picture of how good someone is just by asking him or her. And this is assuming that the person answers honestly. It does not even include the issues of faking and cheating.

So what about asking others?

Asking Others

Unfortunately, similar issues exist when asking others how good someone is. Indeed, if the literature showing difficulties with self-ratings is substantial, it is dwarfed by the research into the challenges of rating others.

It seems to be something that people are capable of: there is evidence that the ratings we make of others can accurately reflect their performance levels. Yet almost all of the rating biases that affect our ability to rate ourselves also apply to rating others, and there are more too. You may have heard of some of these, such as the halo effect.[7] This is where our ratings of individuals' specific qualities are influenced by our overall impression of them. It is why we tend to rate the performance of people we like or find attractive more highly than that of people we do not. It is also why almost everyone—even the professional assessor—tends to rate the performance of senior leaders more highly than that of lower-level managers.[8]

Other biases may be less familiar. For instance, it is obvious that we need to know someone or at least have had a chance to observe a person to rate his or her ability at something. What it less clear is that knowing people can hinder the accuracy of our judgments too. Studies differ in their opinion about how long we need to know someone before this bias comes into effect. But after somewhere between eighteen months and five years, we appear to lose our ability to rate others' performance objectively.[9]

Many biases seem to be culturally based and unconscious: we are simply not aware of them. We appear to rate those similar to ourselves more highly even when we are not aware that they are similar to us (e.g., if they have the same personality profile).[10] Then there is the fact that we are overly influenced by first impressions, preconceptions, and stereotypes: we make up our minds too quickly and tend to hear only the information that reinforces our initial impressions. And topping this off is the irony that despite all of this, we are generally overconfident in our judgments about others.[11]

So as with self-ratings, the ratings of others can be accurate, but they are notoriously unreliable. No matter how objective and free of bias we like to think we are, the sober fact is that we usually are not. Indeed, given all the issues, you could be forgiven for thinking that it is amazing that anyone ever rates anything accurately. Yet we do. We often just need a bit of help.

Eight Less Biased Methods for Measuring Talent or Fit

This is where more formal and structured measurement methods come into play. They are designed to try to minimize the impact of the biases and limitations that plague all our core sources of information about talent. We will look at eight of the most common methods:

- Tools for sifting candidates
- Interviews
- Psychometric tests
- Assessment centers
- Situational judgment tests
- Individual psychological assessment
- 360-degree feedback
- Work sample tests, simulations, and games

To understand how effective each method is, we will look not only at its predictive validities, but also at how it helps us overcome the basic challenges of bias. And as for where to begin, let us start with what for many talent measurement processes is the beginning: tools for sifting candidates.

Sifting Tools

Almost all selection processes involve a kind of funnel. You start with a long list of applicants, potentially thousands of them, and then gradually narrow the list. At this stage, the purpose of talent measurement is to identify the candidates who stand the best chance of ultimately being selected.

This sifting process is often a collection of different methods. To minimize expense and speed things up, companies typically begin with low-cost methods that require little human interaction. Reviewing résumés is almost always part of this process, and telephone interviews and psychometrics are common.[12]

The automated résumé checkers and application form scoring systems that have emerged over the past decade or so are grabbing the headlines in this area. As their names suggest, checkers look directly as people's résumés, while application scorers review information that candidates enter into online forms. Both involve candidates' providing information, which is then rated according to a preprogrammed algorithm or scoring system. These algorithms often include so-called killer items—factors such as work visa status that can result in the immediate rejection of the candidate. Other items or questions can be weighted according to the demands of the role.

In our experience, these systems are popular because they are fast and efficient and because the use of mechanical algorithms tends to be seen as fair. There are some limitations and downsides, of course. Initial setup costs can be high. And these systems do not provide the level of candidate experience that most companies wish to offer their senior-level applicants. In fact, candidates at every level hate long application forms, yet a common mistake we see is for firms to collect more information than they need. There is also the issue that automated systems can reduce diversity because they can exclude candidates with nontraditional backgrounds.

Three developments in sifting are of note. First, companies are increasingly using self-selection. They are open and clear about selection criteria so that those who know that they cannot pass may elect not to apply. Second is the growth of online reference checkers, which are effectively 360-degree feedback tools. They make checking references quick and easy, to the extent that some firms are including checkers in their sifting process. These tools are undeniably attractive and impressive. Yet it remains to be seen whether they will help firms overcome the perennial issue of references: the poor quality of information they provide.

Finally, there is a tendency among some organizations to use information from Facebook, LinkedIn, and other online social networks. It appears to be quite common: a 2012 survey found that 29 percent of firms thought that candidate information on social media sites can be useful.[13] Our views on this are straightforward: checking public sites designed for corporate use, such as LinkedIn, seems entirely natural and no more useful or harmful than looking at a résumé. However, some firms have gone further and are now asking candidates to supply their Facebook passwords so that recruiters can review the site content. If you are thinking of doing this, our advice is simple: do not. It has become a legal and political issue in the United States and other countries, as complaints have been made that it breaches personal privacy. Laws to prevent this practice have already been introduced by some US states, and others are likely to follow suit. Even putting aside the legal and moral issues, there is no evidence that this is an effective way to predict performance in the workplace.

Purely on the basis of their efficiency, sifting tools will continue to be a prominent component of many firms' hiring processes. Their automated aspect reduces the impact of rating biases and thereby improves accuracy. Yet these tools are only as

---

Sifting Tools

When to use: In the early stages of a recruitment process. Automated tools may be useful when you have a large number of candidates and the budget for initial setup costs.

Potential benefits: Can enable you effectively and efficiently to narrow down a large pool of applicants to only those most likely to succeed.

Caveats and concerns: The scoring formula needs to be effective in order for the system to work, and this can take time and effort to ensure. Research is lacking into the predictive accuracy of these systems, and they may have a negative impact on the diversity of successful candidates.

good as the scoring systems they use, so the challenge is how to get this scoring right. Unfortunately, the importance of this is sometimes overlooked, or it is masked by the sleek interfaces of these shiny new systems. Moreover, for the moment, independent research into whether they can indeed deliver the benefits that they promise is lacking. Caution and a careful eye to results are thus recommended.

Interviews

Today interviews are the most used measurement method, probably because of the natural desire to want to meet people before making a decision about them.[14] Research has shown that interviews done well can lead to accurate judgments. They tend to be used to measure competencies and seem to measure different things from intelligence and personality tests, since they can offer incremental validity over them.[15] Yet interviews are based on social interaction and the rating of others, so they are open to all sorts of biases. This means that they can be unreliable as a source of information since interviewers can vary considerably in how they rate the same candidate.[16]

For example, an intriguing fact about all types of interviews is that whatever their stated purpose, they usually do not in fact appear to measure competencies. Interviewers may think that they do and make competency ratings based on them. Yet in most cases, what they seem to be judging candidates on is really a mixture of how socially skilled the candidates are and the degree to which they have done the type of job before.[17] Moreover, from our own research, we know that this seems to be the case regardless of how much training the interviewer has had. Even professional assessors have the same issue. It appears that we have a natural tendency to home in on particular things, such as how intelligent or likable people are. We then base our judgments on these factors rather than on the competencies that we are supposed to be measuring.

To counter the biases inherent in interviews, researchers have found that the best solution is to add structure. In fact, one study has described fifteen separate components of structure. The most common are things like providing scripted questions and banning spontaneous follow-up questions.[18] Adding structure does not seem to do much about the issue of not measuring competencies, but it does seem to make interviewers more able to predict performance. In fact, some studies have suggested that structure can double the validity of interviews, from the 0.14 found for unstructured formats up to 0.35.[19] This is better than most personality tests. Moreover, structure seems to reduce the opportunity for faking or impression management by candidates, while also reducing the likelihood of claims of unfairness and subsequent litigation.[20]

As a result of this research, the past twenty years have witnessed a sea change in interviewing as companies have moved to increasingly structured formats. There are many different types, but two main formats have emerged. There are *competency-based interviews*, which involve a series of questions about specific job-related competencies. You will recognize these from their trademark questions: "Describe a time when you . . ." or, "Give me an example of when you . . ." Then there are *situational interviews*, which ask questions about hypothetical situations, along the lines of, "What would you do if . . ."

There has been much debate about which type is better, and the evidence is mixed. Generally the finding has been that questions about what people have done enable you to make more accurate judgments than hypothetical questions about what they might do.[21] There is also some suggestion that situational interviews may measure problem solving as much as anything else and thus offer lower incremental validity over intelligence tests.[22]

Yet despite near evangelical enthusiasm for structure from some proponents, the approach does have critics. For starters, competency-based interviews may be fine for lower-level jobs, but for higher-level roles, they do not offer a good enough candidate experience. Even for more junior jobs, if such interviews are too strictly structured, they can amount to little more than an oral examination. Indeed, interviews that discourage the use of unscripted questions risk ruining the key benefit of interviews: the opportunity to engage with the candidate as an individual.

Researchers often complain about many managers' reluctance to add structure to their interviews. This betrays a lack of understanding among researchers about how managers use interviews. Researchers have largely focused on making interviews more able to predict performance. But business interviewers also tend to use them to get a sense of the degree of fit or chemistry that exists between the candidate and the business. And, interestingly, there is evidence that skilled interviewers can gauge this sort of thing pretty well.[23]

Rounding all this off is emerging evidence that a bias among researchers toward publishing studies that are positive about structured interviews may have led to an overestimation of how good they are.[24] For this reason, many companies prefer what are called semistructured interviews. These try to impose some kind of structure on proceedings, while also allowing interviewers to ask spontaneous questions. One example is biographical interviews, which explore candidates' past, usually by following a résumé and asking questions about each job.

Although semistructured interviews may not minimize the impact of bias quite as well as a fully structured interview, these formats can still improve predictive accuracy.[25] And, critically, they do not rob interviews of the other benefits that they can provide. However, because semistructured interviews are more open to bias than fully structured ones, they require greater skill to conduct reliably well. This means that businesses need to be able and willing to train their staff in interviewing skills. Unfortunately, in our experience, this is something that is often overlooked.

As a result, firms can fail to make the most of the opportunity that interviews present. Indeed, *we* regard interviews as one of the biggest lost opportunities in talent measurement at present. We hinted at this in chapter 4 when we argued that businesses should be more explicit about measuring aspects of fit. We have seen other examples of lost opportunities in interviews, too, such as the use of panel interviews. Each interviewer is often provided with training or guidance about his or her role, but there is less input on how interviewers should interact with one another to make the best judgments. This is especially important given the evidence that groups of people can be worse at making decisions than individuals.[26] Multiplying the number of interviewers does not guarantee a better outcome.

In chapter 7, therefore, we look further into what businesses can do to make the most of the opportunities that interviews present and enhance the accuracy and reliability of this most fundamental of measurement methods.

Interviews

When to use: In all talent measurement processes. In fact, we believe that no one should ever be hired, fired, or promoted without an interview.

Potential benefits: At best, can offer predictive validities of over 0.35. Can also provide incremental validity over intelligence and personality tests. Can be used to predict person-organization, person-team, and person-manager fit, as well as job performance.

Caveats and concerns: Open to many biases and unreliable as a source of data. The best way of reducing bias—adding structure—can also reduce many of the potential benefits of interviews if too much is added. The best compromise solution—the semistructured interview—requires training if it is to be done well.

Psychometrics

For many people, talent measurement is synonymous with psychometrics. Strictly speaking, this includes all forms of psychological measurement. To most people, though, *psychometrics* refers to those questionnaire-based tests of things like intelligence, personality, and integrity. Some of them are tests of performance (such as intelligence measures), but most involve people rating themselves in response to questions. This opens the tests to rating biases. Yet by carefully selecting which questions are asked and asking them in certain ways, well-constructed tests can reduce the impact of these biases and achieve good levels of accuracy.

In spite of this, suspicion persists. Studies show that managers place more value on information about candidates when it is gained from interviews than when it is measured by psychometrics.[27] They seem to trust their instincts more than the science. Some of this suspicion stems from lingering concerns about faking and cheating. Another issue is concern about the quality of some psychometric tests: some people are just not convinced that they work. And, frankly, who can blame them for their doubts?

Many people can remember the computer-generated reports of a decade ago that attempted to provide some interpretation of scores. Users initially liked the reports because they helped them understand the results. Yet at times, these reports appeared to be not much better than a horoscope. Moreover, over the past ten years, there has been a massive surge in the number of tests available on the market. The challenge for businesses—and what threatens to undermine the psychometric industry—is that although some tests are excellent, many are very poor, and organizations can have a hard time telling the difference. As we reported in chapter 1, only a small proportion of test publishers engage in proper validity studies.[28]

In chapter 5, we consider how businesses can navigate these issues when choosing tools. For now, what is important is that although there are doubts and concerns, the use of psychometric tests appears to be growing. The bottom line is that they are relatively quick, cheap, and effective. They are seen as an easy win.

Psychometrics has changed a lot over the years. One of the biggest developments was the introduction of first computerized and then online testing. Some people initially questioned whether these tests were equivalent to the old pencil-and-paper versions, but subsequent research has shown that this is not really a problem.[29] Others also expressed concern that online tests are more prone to disruptions that can affect people's performance.[30] Yet studies on the impact of this differ in their view of how significant it is.[31]

The reality is that computerized and online testing have made testing easier and better by allowing remote testing and the collection of bigger databases. They also allow vendors to do some interesting new things with their tests. They can, for instance, now measure aspects of how people are taking the test, such as how long each question takes, which can help identify cheating. And the very latest tests are beginning to include high-fidelity item presentation—that is, the use of video clips and animations.

A second major development has been the rise of new ways of scoring tests, such as computerized adaptive testing. Although they differ in approach, these new scoring methods all attempt to do the same thing: get more information from fewer questions. With traditional psychometrics, test takers answer a set of predetermined questions. But with computerized adaptive testing, the test adapts to individual test takers. If they get a question wrong, it gives them an easier one the next time; if they get the question right, it gives them a harder one next. This allows the test to home in on someone's level of ability quickly. Organizations are generally enthusiastic about these innovations, too, as they allow briefer tests. Indeed, the days of the hour-long personality test seem numbered in the face of new tests claiming to offer similar validities in just twenty minutes.

Indeed, one easy conclusion would be that no other method offers the same level of accuracy and reliability in such a short time and at so little cost. Yet there is a sting in the tail here because psychometrics has a hidden weak spot, and it is a big one. Although some vendors claim that the usefulness of a test lies in its validity levels, we heartily disagree. The utility of a test is determined by what is done with it. And the harsh reality is that the way many businesses use psychometrics leaves much to be desired. The results are often either ignored or overly revered as definitive measurements that capture all the complexities that it is worth knowing about people.

Some of this misuse stems from the suspicions we mentioned earlier about quality and reliability. But some of it results from a simple lack of understanding about how best to use the data. In chapter 7, we return to look at this issue and what you can and cannot do with measurement results. Psychometric tests may be the epitome of talent measurement and a key part of its future, but they need to be handled with care.

Psychometrics

When to use: In all talent measurement processes. Tests of ability and intelligence tend to be used earlier in selection processes. Tests of personality, values, and attitudes tend to be used later in the assessment, typically in combination with an interview.

Potential benefits: Relatively quick, cheap, and accurate.

Caveats and concerns: Many of the psychometrics on the market lack proper research to validate their accuracy, and it can be difficult to know which tests work and which do not. In addition, psychometric results need more work and more careful handling than the outputs of many other measurement processes.

Assessment Centers

Assessment centers have long been held up as the gold standard of talent measurement. In their classic format, they involve multiple assessors who are observing a group of participants over a series of exercises and tests and rating them on a number of competencies. Effectively, then, they are a collection of other methods, yet they are also more than the sum of their parts. By involving both test scores and multiple assessor ratings, they seem able to minimize the impact of rater biases and produce reliable judgments.[32] They thus appear to enable good predictive judgments, with reported validities of around 0.40.[33] This is higher than interviews and personality tests but lower than intelligence tests.

The German military of the 1920s is widely credited with starting the assessment center concept as a way of selecting soldiers, although the term was coined in the 1930s by a Harvard professor. It was not until the 1970s that assessment centers really caught on in businesses, though. Best practice in how to develop and run them is now well documented, and there are numerous books on the subject. But over the years, three particularly interesting issues have emerged.

First, assessment centers are designed to measure competencies. Yet there is now a substantial body of evidence that shows that, like interviews, they may often not actually do so. Evidence suggests, then, that although assessors may appear to measure different competencies, what they are often seeing and actually rating is overall performance in each exercise.[34] For example, an assessor may be tasked when observing a group discussion exercise with rating the participants on a number of competencies, such as assertiveness and communication skills. Yet statistical analyses show that more often than not, even though they may give separate ratings to these two competencies, what they are really assessing is the ability to do well in a discussion exercise.

The practical implication is that when you choose or develop assessment centers, you should focus not so much on how they measure particular competencies, but on what exercises they use and their relevance to what you are trying to measure.

Second, assessment centers do not seem to work as well as they used to. Validity levels seem to be falling, with a recent meta-analysis reporting levels of around 0.27.[35] If this is true, then assessment centers have lost a quarter of their predictive power in a decade. A number of different theories as to why this is happening have been suggested, but the most convincing is that the quality of assessment centers seems to be declining. Some researchers are concerned about increasing use of off-the-shelf centers that are not sufficiently tailored to organizations' needs. Others cite the disturbingly high number of competencies that many centers seem to try to measure. A recent study, for instance, found that nearly a quarter rate eleven or more competencies, and over three-quarters use five or fewer exercises to do so.[36] Finally, a number of concerns have been raised about the lack of training provided to assessors.

As with any other product, if its development is distributed across a range of unregulated suppliers, the quality of each supplier's work will vary, and the overall quality of the product will inevitably fall. In our view, this is precisely what has happened with assessment centers. As with psychometrics, it can be difficult to know when you are getting a quality product. Yet it is not only the market that is at fault. Cost pressures in implementing assessment centers frequently mean that businesses compromise on their development and deployment. These compromises are understandable, but each one chips away at the validity of the assessment center.

The third issue is a very recent one: the use of assessment centers appears to be declining rapidly, particularly in the United States. The forces driving this seem to be the increasing availability of virtual methods such as psychometric testing and online interviews and a desire to reduce costs. The travel costs associated with bringing all the participants to one place seem to be a particular concern for many businesses, especially in a tough economic climate.

One thing to be careful of here is that some of the new online measurement processes that are emerging as alternatives are calling themselves assessment centers even though they are not (because they do not include group exercises). They are simply trying to cash in on assessment centers' good name. This is not to say that all the tools being used to replace assessment centers are poor, of course, and at the end of this chapter, a small case study describes one such effective alternative.

So assessment centers, once held up as an aspirational pinnacle, appear to be in decline. Given the falling standards associated with them, this may not be a bad thing. Yet we would be sad to see them go because, done well, they present a unique opportunity to evaluate talent in a rigorous setting.

Assessment Centers

When to use: In all selection methods. Tend to be used at more junior levels as an assessment process and at more senior levels as a developmental process.

Potential benefits: Rigorous process that provides multiple perspectives on individuals and an opportunity to see them interacting with colleagues. Can be accurate and reliable when done properly.

Caveats and concerns: To deliver the validities that they are capable of, they need to be done properly, without too many compromises.

Situational Judgment Tests

Although they have been around since the 1920s, situational judgment tests (SJTs) feel relatively new. They were little used for many years, until computerized testing arrived in the 1990s and opened up new possibilities for them. Sometimes called *low-fidelity simulations*, they entail presenting people with realistic work scenarios and then asking questions about them. The scenarios can be presented as written descriptions, videos, or animations, and answers are selected from a multiple-choice list. Some situational judgment tests can adapt to the test taker too, in that responses to one scenario determine which situation is presented next. Many firms like this approach since it means that test takers are presented with the consequences of their choices.

Situational judgment tests have traditionally been built around critical incidents and ask a range of questions about how to respond to them. This type of SJT is still often used for assessing job knowledge, like safety procedures or customer service behaviors. More recently, though, we have also seen the rise of SJTs that try to measure things such as problem solving or aspects of personality.

There has been a fair amount of debate about which type of SJT is superior and how best to develop these tests. For example, two main types of questions can be asked. Some tests ask people about behavioral tendencies—how they tend to respond to situations. Others, known as knowledge-based tests, ask people to select the correct or best response to a situation.[37] The jury is still out on which is more effective. Behavioral tendency SJTs seem to offer greater incremental validity over intelligence tests and appear to measure what a candidate can do when performing at her or his best. Knowledge-based SJTs appear less easy to fake and cheat on and seem to measure typical performance levels.[38]

Situational judgment tests are increasingly popular for two main reasons. First, they look valid, appear fair and relevant, and tend to evoke few complaints. Next, they *are* fairly valid. A review of ninety-five studies found validities for SJTs of around 0.34—about the same as a good personality test.[39] However, the review also found a lot of variability between tests, and in our experience this is certainly the case. Good tests can be really good, but poor tests can be really poor. The key to quality is simple: how well constructed the scenarios and multiple-choice responses are. A poor test will present scenarios that are not that relevant to what is being measured and offer multiple-choice answers that are obvious. A good SJT poses complex, relevant situations and a choice of responses—a number of which could be correct.

Situational judgment tests have also been shown to provide some incremental validity over both intelligence and personality tests. The extra validity is not large, since SJTs tend to measure aspects of both intelligence and personality, but it is there. So if you already use a combination of intelligence and personality tests, SJTs will not typically provide anything extra. However, if you currently use only an intelligence test, adding an SJT will give you roughly the same extra validity as adding a personality test (around 0.07).[40]

In light of this, you might well wonder why SJTs are not more popular. In our experience, the answer is simple: time and money. Developing a good SJT requires both, since developing the scenarios and questions requires the input of subject matter experts. There are also issues with shelf-life, as some tests may remain useful only for a few years. And for global companies, the need to localize the tests for different geographies can add considerable cost. Given all this, for many companies that already use an intelligence test, adding a personality tool seems quicker, easier, and cheaper.

The use of situational judgment tests has thus largely remained confined to two instances. The first is large-scale recruitment drives, for which the numbers of candidates can justify the costs. We have recently seen some interesting examples of this in retail and customer-service businesses using video-based SJTs. The second is where the testing of specific skills is deemed important. In training needs analysis, for example, a company may have to identify whether employees require training in safety-related issues.

So situational judgment tests are a mixed bag. Sometimes they are not worth the effort. But if you have the right need and the commitment to develop them well, they can be hard to beat.

Situational Judgment Tests

When to use: Training needs analyses or large-scale recruitment drives, preferably confined to particular geographies.

Potential benefits: Easy to run, since the automated process can be completed virtually. Viewed as fair and can offer good levels of validity.

Caveats and concerns: Need to be well designed to deliver the described benefits and may need more maintenance and ongoing development than some other methods.

Individual Psychological Assessment

The dark horse of talent measurement is individual psychological assessment. For starters, it is rarely called that, since every vendor calls its proprietary version of it something different. It is also the least researched method of all, and any independent studies that do exist are generally not that positive. In fact, if you ask most researchers, they would probably dismiss individual psychological assessment as being of dubious validity and value. Yet it has been used in organizations for over thirty years and is a significant part of the measurement market. And despite the lack of positive research, it is also one of the methods that businesses most often choose to use with their senior executives.

Individual psychological assessment can vary in what specifically it entails, but it is a bit like an individual assessment center and is usually used to assess competencies. It typically involves an interview and some psychometric tests, and some vendors add a simulation exercise or presentation. It always results in a report written by the assessor about the individual assessed. This tends to contain a description of personal characteristics—strengths, weaknesses, and ratings of abilities with regard to certain competencies.

The popularity of individual psychological assessment is probably explained by two things. First, it can offer a good experience for the participant. It is very personal, can leave the individual feeling heard and understood, and can have a developmental feel to it. Second, it can offer a good experience for the business. Unlike psychometrics reports, the results are interpreted, and the business often has a chance to speak with the assessor and ask questions about the findings. This personal service does not come cheap. Yet given the cost of poor hiring decisions, many businesses see individual psychological assessment as a good investment and effective risk management, especially for senior leaders.

So what does the research say? One review of validity studies found that the average validity of individual psychological assessments in predicting performance was around 0.26 (just below personality psychometrics). However, validities were higher when individual psychological assessments were used for assessing managers (0.47) than for both technical experts (0.24) and all other groups (0.16).[41]

Unfortunately, there is not much independent research on the matter. In fact, a major review identified only twenty studies, of which eighteen were conducted during the 1950s and 1960s.[42] The reason for this is that the number of people going through individual psychological assessment in each business tends to be fairly small, so obtaining enough results to enable a good analysis of validity is tough.[43] Complicating matters is the fact that each vendor tends to have its own approach to doing individual psychological assessment. And, of course, for a vendor even to conduct a study, it needs to access the performance scores of the people assessed, which can be difficult.

Yet what concerns researchers most about individual psychological assessment is not so much whether it can be used to predict performance, but its reliability in doing so. For example, one classic study asked three assessors to each independently assess the same three candidates. It found a high level of disagreement over both specific attributes and overall job suitability. And when fifty other assessors were then asked to review the assessment results, only one-third of them agreed with the original psychologists' judgments.[44]

Given that the outputs of individual psychological assessment rely solely on the assessor's expertise, it is not really a surprise that great variation is found. After all, professional assessors are open to the same rating biases and judgment errors as everyone else. So the conclusion seems to be that with a good assessor and a good process, individual psychological assessment can be very effective in accurately describing people and predicting performance. But as methods go, it is unreliable. Assessors vary considerably in their ability, and working out which are the good ones is not easy.

Despite this, our experience is that once organizations start using individual assessments, they keep doing so. They like them and believe that they are adding value. They can be used to provide clear and objective comparisons of individuals. They can be used to identify potential risks in hiring or promoting someone. And they can provide a guide for managing and developing individuals. Moreover, of all the measurement methods, individual psychological assessment is the one that probably has the best potential for helping evaluate individuals' level of fit with a business, team, or manager. Of course, whether it currently and typically achieves all these things is another matter altogether.

Indeed, in our view, to minimize the downsides and deliver the potential benefits, individual psychological assessment probably needs more careful management by businesses than any other method. Yet what we tend to find is altogether different. All too often, businesses find a vendor they trust and then hand the process over to it. In chapter 8, we return to this issue when we look at how to manage vendors, and in the appendix we provide a brief guide to choosing a vendor for individual psychological assessments.

Individual Psychological Assessment

When to use: Mid- to senior-level selection or development processes.

Potential benefits: Personal service for participants, excellent opportunity to assess aspects of fit, and results that are tailored to and interpreted for businesses.

Caveats and concerns: Validity of the process is dependent on the quality of the assessor. It thus needs closer ongoing management by the business to ensure effectiveness than any other measurement method.

360-Degree Feedback

As its name suggests, 360-degree feedback involves asking a range of people who interact with an individual to rate or answer questions about him or her. These questions are usually designed to measure either performance levels or certain competencies. The method has its roots in military selection practices from World War II, when selectors found that the inclusion of peer evaluations improved predictions of future performance. The practice moved to the US corporate sector in the 1950s, grew in the 1960s and 1970s, and became popular internationally in the 1980s. It is now an established practice within many, if not most, medium to large organizations. It is mostly used with management populations and for either personal development or as part of performance management or talent identification processes.

This feedback is popular because it is seen as fair and valid and because both businesses and participants tend to like it. It is often viewed as a way for managers and peers to give direct feedback in a safe, nonconfrontational way. Moreover, after a study found that subordinates' appraisals of managers could be as predictive of performance as assessment center ratings, 360s have been touted as a cheap and effective alternative.[45] How good are they really, though? After all, 360s are open to the whole gamut of rating biases, and it is not obvious what they do to mitigate the impact of them.

In terms of personal development, the picture does not initially look good. For example, a review of other studies found that the actual impact of 360-degree feedback in improving performance was limited.[46] In our experience, though, this is not because 360s cannot aid performance improvement. Instead, it is usually the result of one of three things: a poor tool, poor motivation on the part of the participant, or poor implementation by the business. As with psychometrics, some tools are better than others, and it can be difficult to work out which are the good ones. In addition, 360s depend on participants to make something of them and develop themselves, and firms often do not do enough to support this. Yet 360-degree feedback can succeed as a tool for development only when all three of these issues are addressed.

As for using 360s to assist in performance management and talent spotting, the advice typically given is to avoid doing so. What tends to happen is that either 360-degree feedback reports are given to managers to help inform appraisal ratings, or a mathematical formula is used to help generate performance ratings from the 360s. However, 360s have to overcome all the normal rating biases, which can undermine their effectiveness in two ways.

First, the ratings can fail to distinguish high performers from poor performers, since almost everyone scores high. When we look at how people rate, we find that they generally overrate others' effectiveness and do not use the whole of the rating scale.[47] And when feedback givers think their ratings will be shared with a manager or used for performance management, their ratings go up even further and become less predictive of performance.[48] For example, when given a scale of 1 to 5, they may primarily use ratings of 3, 4, and 5. In one business we worked with, the result of this was that the average rating was 4.74 out of 5.

Second, 360-degree ratings can be unreliable at distinguishing what each individual's strengths and weaknesses are. We know this because when we analyze 360-degree data, we find that it is extremely susceptible to the halo effect, whereby people are rated high or low on all competencies. In other words, 360s often measure just one thing: "How much I like you" or "How much I rate you."

In our experience, the vast majority of organizations do not have a culture of giving open and direct feedback. As a result, the two factors we just described tend to significantly distort 360-degree ratings. Many vendors have focused on developing techniques to try to reduce the impact of these biases, for example, by introducing special ways of asking questions and different types of rating scales. Some of these can help, but only to a limited extent. We do not mean to say that 360s cannot be useful in performance appraisals; we are just saying that the conditions need to be right, and often they are not.

To try to circumvent these issues, a few vendors are trying to reinvent 360s and have come up with fundamentally different designs for them. One of these approaches involves rating people not on a traditional low-to-high type scale, but on a scale that runs from "underdeveloped competency" to "overused strength."[49] This is an interesting approach since it does not assume that the more you display a certain behavior, the better it is. A similar approach entails categorizing competencies, putting them in boxes such as "underused behavior" and "overused behavior." Finally, an approach that we have personally developed involves ranking behaviors or competencies rather than rating them. This forces people to distinguish between strengths and weakness and prevents them from overrating.

Moreover, one interesting stream of research is studies showing that the biggest predictor of performance is not how highly people are rated, but the degree of alignment between self-ratings and others' ratings. People who overestimate their abilities tend to have the highest development needs and the lowest performance levels, whereas people who are rated highly by both themselves and others tend to be better performers.[50] Thus 360-degree systems that focus on this alignment, rather than only on how highly people are rated, are likely to be far more effective in both predicting success and helping people identify potential performance derailers. The one caveat is that most of the research on this to date has come out of the United States and Europe, and further research needs to be done on how cultural factors may affect the likelihood of ratings by self and others being aligned.

360-Degree Feedback

When to use: In personal development processes and as part of performance appraisal or talent management.

Potential benefits: Enables constructive feedback directly focused on performance improvement issues. Generally liked and valued by participants.

Caveats and concerns: Effectiveness as a development tool depends on the quality of the tool, motivation of the user, and support from the business. Utility for performance appraisal is likely to be strongly undermined when businesses do not already have a culture of open and honest feedback.

So 360s can assist both personal development and performance management, but as with all the other methods, only when they are implemented properly and with a careful eye on the factors that can undermine their effectiveness. Indeed, 360s are particularly vulnerable to rating biases, and we are concerned that businesses often seem unaware of just how much these can distort results. New tools are being developed in an effort to sidestep some of these issues, but only time will tell if they are effective solutions.

Work Sample Tests, Simulations, and Games

Work sample tests have been around for a long time. They involve, quite simply, giving people a sample of work and then seeing how they do. They are generally seen as fair and very capable of predicting performance. They are also relatively free from rating biases since actual performance can be measured. Validities can vary a lot between tests, but figures from 0.33 to 0.54 have been reported.[51] This means that they account for anywhere between 10 and 30 percent of the causes of success and can even be as predictive as intelligence tests. They are typically used for skilled and semiskilled jobs, and each test tends to be specific to certain roles and tasks.

We include four main types of measurement method in this group. First, there are work sample tests, such as key stroke tests for data entry clerks or physical fitness tests in the military. We also include the increasing use, in lower-level roles, of job probationary periods as tests of whether someone can perform well.

Second are the simulation exercises often used as part of a bigger measurement process, such as an assessment center. These typically involve role-playing exercises in which participants participate in a simulation of a meeting. Alternatively, in what are called in-tray or e-tray exercises, participants are asked to respond to reports, e-mails, or phone calls about a particular project or series of issues. Role plays done well can involve professional actors, and some of the e-tray products available are very elaborate and include video and audio.

Simulations can be effective, but they need to be well designed and to mimic the work environment accurately. It has been suggested that role plays favor extroverts, and many people report a strong dislike of role plays, even when they may be for personal development purposes. And e-tray exercises may be more of an alternative measure of intelligence than anything else (and so offer little incremental validity over intelligence tests).

Third, there are internships, which are increasingly being used as a way of testing graduate and entry-level new hires. Companies are thus intentionally hiring more people than they ultimately need, with an eye to selecting the best based on actual job performance. This may seem harsh from a young job hunter's perspective, but it involves real work, and it is hard to argue that it is not fair.

Finally, there are the games that are garnering all the headlines these days. Google, Facebook, L'Oréal, Microsoft, hotel and resort chain Harrah's, and the US Air Force have all run online contests to identify potential new employees. One company we recently worked with ran an online contest to identify potential graduate traders, which immersed the would-be traders in an intensive, simulated trading environment. These types of methods are popular because they can provide publicity, boost a brand, and deliver an accurate measure of talent all at the same time. It is not hard to see their attractiveness. However, they may require regular updating, can often be applied to only specific roles, and there is a lack of solid evidence on how effective they really are.

In general, then, work sample tests are to be applauded. However, they do need to be well designed and can be quite costly given their relatively limited applicability.

> ## Work Sample Tests
>
> *When to use:* In recruitment processes, often for skilled or
>   semiskilled roles.
>
> *Potential benefits:* When well designed, cannot be beaten
>   for perceived fairness and legal defensibility and may also
>   be good predictors of performance.
>
> *Caveats and concerns:* Effectiveness depends on design and
>   the relevance of the test to the skills required for an
>   individual to succeed in the role. Simply adding a
>   generic role-play exercise is not likely to deliver much
>   value.

Summary

Almost all of the eight methods we have looked at have to
contend with the same rating biases that are present when we
just ask individuals or their managers how good they are. Yet all
of them are capable of helping us to deal with these biases and
arriving at more accurate judgments.

We could have added a ninth category: integrated tools.
These are mostly online, are called different things by different
vendors, and combine various combinations of the eight core
methods to produce bigger tools. They may, for example, contain
a combination of psychometrics and an online simulation exercise. These are not bespoke measurement processes specifically
designed for individual businesses, but ready-made, off-the-shelf,
Web-based solutions. They have the advantage of being relatively cost-efficient and tend to have good validities because they
combine measures. However, many of them have only a limited
ability to be tailored to the needs of individual businesses and
offer little, if any, assessment of the different types of fit. So

although they are undoubtedly an interesting development, we are concerned by their focus on benchmarking and one-size-fits-all approach. Nonetheless, these integrated tools may still suit some situations, and it is worth keeping an eye on them. If they can be developed to measure all four types of fit, they could form a large part of measurement's future.

In the meantime, one major question remains. How do you choose which of the eight core methods to use? It is to this issue that we turn in the next chapter.

CASE STUDY

Replacing Assessment Centers with Virtual Measurement

There is a rapidly increasing trend to replace assessment centers with cheaper alternatives. Yet cheaper is not always better and is particularly concerning when it comes to measurement. This is because less expensive measurement processes invariably involve compromises that entail a reduction in validity. And if you reduce validity too much, a measurement process can easily become next to worthless.

Compromise can be done well, though. Consider the recent experience of a US-based multinational. It had historically used assessment centers to assess and develop its leaders. However, as the economic downturn began to be felt, this was no longer economically viable given the significant travel costs that could be incurred. So it looked to develop an online alternative and approached the vendor CEB-Valtera for a solution.

The company had a fairly large competency framework, so the first thing that CEB-Valtera did was to work with the firm to narrow the list of competencies to a more manageable number: only the most relevant were chosen. This made sure that the accuracy of the results would not be diluted by trying to measure too many things, while also keeping the time required to complete the process to a minimum.

CEB-Valtera then identified four measures that would allow it to assess each of the six chosen competencies at multiple points: an intelligence test, a personality psychometric, an online structured interview with an assessor, and a new measure that it developed especially for the process—a multirater situational judgment test. It was like a 360-degree feedback tool in that it asked people who worked with the individuals being assessed to provide information about how they typically acted. But rather than asking feedback givers to provide ratings, it asked them to answer multiple-choice questions about how individuals tended to respond in certain situations. As an output, it provided scores against each of the competencies being measured.

It is too early tell the predictive power of this process or whether it will match the predictive validity that an assessment center might have provided. Yet there is every reason to hope it is effective. For starters, it combines measurement methods, each carefully chosen in part for the incremental validity it could offer over the others. In addition, although it contains generic intelligence and personality measures, it also contains measures that were designed to evaluate the level of fit between individuals and the needs of the company. It might not have quite the level of validity of a great assessment center, but it is a rigorous process with the potential to offer good validities and comes with substantial cost savings.

One final thing. Ask almost any assessor, and she will tell you that she prefers interviewing people face-to-face and that "something is lost" when interviewing online. For that reason, many prefer to avoid it. Yet as Nancy Tippins, senior vice president at CEB-Valtera, notes, people in multinational businesses often have to work virtually. So in this respect, an online interview can provide a realistic simulation of the working environment.

5

CHOOSING THE BEST METHODS AND TOOLS FOR YOUR BUSINESS

The eight methods we described in chapter 4 address the challenges of talent measurement in eight different ways. But how does a business choose among them? Chapter 4 provided insights into the various strengths and weaknesses of the methods themselves. In this chapter, we look at how your organization's specific concerns and needs should guide your choice of which method to use.

Key Issues in Choosing Tools

For researchers, the critical factor in selecting a method or tool is what works best or has the highest validity. But for businesses, there is always a trade-off between best practices, and other practical and implementation issues tend to lead their choice. In fact, there are seven key issues you should consider when choosing which method or tool to use:

- Your location
- What you want to measure, and why
- Whom you want to assess
- Legal and diversity concerns
- How well a method is likely to work
- How much it costs
- How long it takes

We will look at each of these in turn and present them in a rough logical order, but we do not mean to suggest that any one of them is always more important than the others.

Your Location

The issue of location consists of five smaller, interrelated issues: local traditions, availability, regulatory constraints, portability, and language differences.

First, different countries and regions have different traditions of measurement and preferences for tools, and in a few countries, such as South Africa, there are legal restrictions on which tools you can use. So at a basic level, where you are determines which measurement methods you tend to consider.

References, for example, are one of the most used methods in the United States, yet they are far less popular in parts of Europe, including Spain, Portugal, and the Netherlands. Indeed, Europe is a patchwork of varying practices. Intelligence tests are very popular in Spain and the Netherlands, but far less so in Italy, Norway, and Turkey.[1] Graphology is used in France and by over 15 percent of companies in the German-speaking part of Switzerland, but hardly used anywhere else.[2] Asia is also diverse, though slightly less so than Europe. Interviews are less common in China and South Korea, while selection in Japan tends to emphasize the ability to get on well with others.[3] The Middle East is a little more consistent; there, assessment centers and psychometrics are common. In some South American countries, measurement in general is relatively rare.

A related issue is the tools that are available. In South America, for instance, psychometric tests are generally viewed with caution, largely due to the lack of appropriate, locally developed tests. Similarly, in Brazil, the tests available are mostly international ones, written in international Portuguese rather than Brazilian Portuguese. But availability problems are not only about language. With personality tests, for example, although the questions may be translated, they may not make sense in the local culture. For this reason, there has been a move to develop personality tests that are designed by locals for locals. As an idea, it sounds good, but these local tools often lack the rigor and validity levels of the big internationally developed tests.[4] A global balancing act is therefore required to accommodate both efficacy and local needs.

The third issue is regulatory differences in how tools are used. In the Netherlands, for example, assessment reports about a job applicant need to be shown to the candidate before the business can use them. And in the United Kingdom and South Africa, there are regulatory or legal constraints on who can use psychometrics.

Next is the issue of the portability of particular methods and tools. In our experience, organizations often start with a locally designed measurement process and then try to apply it globally. This can work, but it has risks. A large global bank, for example, recently struggled when it tried to implement a 360-degree feedback process globally. It worked fine in most countries, but in India, employees had a culture of giving managers the feedback that they thought the managers wanted to hear. This drastically reduced the utility of the measure and prevented the firm from comparing the ratings of people in different countries.

Another example comes from a large US-based multinational that committed to using a well-known and highly regarded intelligence test as part of a restructuring process. However, when it used the test internationally, it found that the US and UK versions of the test were not equivalent. In fact, they were different tests, with different types of questions and different levels of difficulty. In the end, the multinational had to use different tools in different countries, which limited its ability to compare people across locations.

Finally, there is the perhaps more hidden issue of needing to accommodate different languages, even within a single country. A few years ago, we helped a UK-based organization choose a test of intelligence for its graduate recruitment process. In doing so, we discovered that people from nine different nationalities and cultural backgrounds were applying.

Since you need to test people in their first language for a test to be accurate, the company had to find a test that could measure intelligence in all nine languages. So just because your business is not global does not mean that you do not need to worry about global issues.

As a result of these five related issues, then, where you are and where you intend to use your measurement methods can have a big impact on which tools you choose. Indeed, for multinationals, the growing globalization of the workforce is making measurement increasingly difficult.

Location: Recommendations

1. *Be aware of local measurement traditions, but try not to be constrained by them.* To find out what the local traditions are, ask a local HR leader or vendor. To gain a sense of other approaches, a useful question might be, "How would you measure this in other countries?"

2. *Always begin by considering the different locations where you might need to use your tools.* You will almost certainly not be able to find one method that suits all locations. But you will at least be able to minimize difficulties and approach them proactively when they do occur.

3. *Do not assume that any tool will be portable to other locations.* Make sure to ask vendors for specific information about the portability of their tools.

4. *Check what languages and nationalities you may need to accommodate.* Even if you are operating in only one location, your employees may have diverse backgrounds.

What You Want to Measure, and Why

In terms of what sign of talent you want to measure, some methods are obviously better suited to certain tasks than others, but there are fewer hard-and-fast rules than you might imagine. If you want to measure prior experience, sifting tools and biodata are probably the best options, although interviews and individual psychological assessment are often used as well. If you wish to measure competencies, assessment centers, interviews, and individual psychological assessments are the usual options (though each has limits, as discussed in chapter 4). If you want to measure intelligence, psychometrics is hard to beat. And if you want to measure personality, psychometrics is once again probably the best option, although most methods can be used. Do not assume there is only one way to measure each factor. And if you are not happy with one method, look at some others.

Regarding why you want to measure—your business purpose— there are six common applications for measurement:

- *Selection*—including both hiring and promotion
- *Capability review and benchmarking*—assessing a group of people in a function or section of a business as part of a restructuring or transformation project
- *Due diligence*—assessing executives and other staff as part of a merger or acquisition
- *Talent fishing*—identifying potential future leaders
- *Development*—assessing people as part of a development process in order to identify their learning needs
- *Performance appraisal*—evaluating people as part of a formal or informal appraisal process

Again, there are few hard-and-fast rules here about which methods best suit each of the six. However, sifting tools are really required only for hiring processes, and only work sample tests, interviews, and 360-degree feedback are generally appropriate for performance appraisals. Beyond this, there is a lot of flexibility in what you can do.

In our experience, there are at least two reasons to think ahead about your purpose for using measurement. First is the type of outputs you require and what you need to do with this information. At a basic level, for example, do you need a detailed report, or are some scores sufficient? For example, you may require a method that can provide detailed developmental suggestions. In this case, individual psychological assessment, 360-degree feedback, or assessment centers might be appropriate. Alternatively, you may need a method that will provide simple scores, such as when testing knowledge or skill. In these situations, situational judgment tests (SJTs) or work sample tests can help.

Second, and critically, the purpose of measurement methods is usually not just to measure things. Measurements tend to fulfill broader functions too. Hiring people is sometimes just about employing the best candidate, but it can also be about increasing the diversity of a firm's talent pool and enhancing the firm's reputation. And to make sure that you obtain a tool that can fulfill these broader needs, you need to be clear and explicit about what they are.

Companies tend to approach vendors and say something like, "We need a selection process," or, "We want to measure intelli-

---

What You Want to Measure, and Why: Recommendations

1. *Be clear on the types of output you need,* what you need to do with the information, and what the measurement process needs to achieve for the business. If you are unsure what you need a measure to do, ask your stakeholders what they want from it.

2. *Check whether a tool can do what you need it to do.* The easiest way to do this is to ask vendors for evidence that it can.

gence." They then ask for evidence of validity. Ideally, though, they should go to the market with a broader and more specific list of requirements. To become discriminating about which method to use, businesses first need to be clear about what they need the tools to do.

Whom You Want to Assess

Just as you need to ensure that your chosen tools can do what you require of them, you also need to ensure that they are appropriate for the audience. Broadly speaking, at junior levels, for example, the challenge for measurement is usually to sift candidates and spot the most talented in a group. With more senior-level and technical people, however, the challenge shifts to be more about trying to discriminate among a small number of highly qualified individuals.

Psychometric tests of intelligence and work sample tests can be excellent as sifting tools. Yet they tend not to add so much value when used with executives.[5] A related issue here is the tenure of individuals. As we noted in chapter 2, intelligence tests can be very predictive of performance in new employees, yet assessments of personality or character are often better predictors of performance in longer-serving employees.[6]

The question of "whom" also relates to an increasing trend for companies to view the people they are measuring as "customers" and therefore to want to use methods that are appealing to them (or at least unoffensive). This appears to be a bigger concern in the Untied States than elsewhere, but it is a growing issue everywhere.[7] It is important because people's perceptions of measurement methods can have a significant impact. In recruitment, for instance, they can influence things like how inclined people are to accept an offer from a company and how likely they are to recommend the business to others.[8] People's perceptions of the methods you use are thus important for your brand. They are also particularly pertinent for companies recruiting to fill roles for which it is hard to attract candidates.

Perhaps surprisingly, there appear to be few cultural differences in people's typical views of different methods. In fact, age, gender, and ethnic background seem to make no difference at all.[9] The methods most liked tend to be either traditional ones, such as interviews, or ones that are clearly job relevant, such as work sample tests.[10] Least favored of all are psychometric measures of integrity and tests based on biodata.

There are a couple of caveats here. First, not all interviews are equally liked. People appear to dislike overly structured ones or being interviewed multiple times and asked the same questions by different interviewers.[11] So the quality of the measure matters. Second, how individuals perceive both their own status and the status of the organization seems important. For instance, people who view themselves as having high status tend to dislike tests of their ability or intelligence more than people who do not see themselves this way. People applying for roles at what they perceive to be a high-status organization, however, appear to be less critical of its selection procedures.[12]

Worth remembering, too, is that how methods are explained, combined, and administered can be just as important as the nature of the test. For example, job applicants asked to take psychometric tests tend to like them more when the reasons for using the tests are clearly explained, there is a balance between the tests and other measurement methods, and the tests did not take more than an hour to complete.[13]

One final thing: people who "fail" or do not do well or are anxious about a particular type of measure tend not to like it.[14] Some people hate interviews, and most people seem to dislike intelligence tests. Yet this does not mean that you should avoid using them if everything else suggests that they are the most appropriate for your needs. When it comes to talent measurement, the customer should definitely not always be king.

Whom You Want to Assess: Recommendations

1. *Make sure the methods you use can discriminate among different levels of the type of talent you wish to measure.* If you are unsure, ask a vendor about this and what your options are.

2. *Think about the participants' experience of the assessment and what methods can do to make it better.* Do not assume it will be good. When seeking a tool from vendors, explicitly ask about this aspect. A lot has to do with communication with participants—letting them know why they are taking the test and what it adds to the process—but some methods are just generally more liked.

Legal and Diversity Concerns

Depending on where you are in the world, legal compliance can be a critical issue in deciding which tools to use. For the most part, it involves making sure that you do not unfairly discriminate against any subgroup in the population—for example, particular ethnic groups, genders, or disabled people. You will often hear this issue referred to as *adverse impact*.

Avoiding adverse impact is an admirable goal for any measurement method. Yet what makes it so important in some countries is the specificity of the laws regulating it and the type of litigation environment. In some territories, the laws are quite vague about what counts as discrimination, and there is not a strong culture of legally challenging decisions. In countries such as the United States and South Africa, however, the situation is very different. The laws that prohibit discrimination are specific about what counts as unfair and place the burden of being able to prove fairness firmly on businesses. Moreover, when a company gets it wrong, the consequences can prove expensive and damaging, especially in environments as litigious as the United States. As a result, US firms introducing new measurement processes typically conduct a study beforehand to prove that measures are fair and predictive of performance.

At a basic level, then, legal compliance is about knowing what you can and cannot do. This may sound simple, but for global businesses, it can be complex because countries differ as to which subgroups are protected and what is illegal. In most territories, treating people differently or selecting a disproportionate number of people from certain groups is enough to count as evidence of discrimination. In a few, however, such as Taiwan and Turkey, evidence of the intent to discriminate is required. In addition, the preferential treatment of subgroups is prohibited by some countries, such as Turkey and the United Kingdom, as well as in some US states. Yet it is permitted in others, such as Belgium and Chile.

Moreover, even if you are well informed about legal requirements, avoiding adverse impact entirely is often not possible. The issue that most typifies this concerns intelligence tests and ethnicity.

Culture, Diversity, and Intelligence Psychometrics. As we showed in chapter 2, intelligence measures are far and away the most predictive of success. Yet no other factor or test has also proved quite as big a cause of adverse impact.

The issue is often presented as simply a matter of "whites do better than blacks." Since the differences between these two groups are widely viewed as the result of social disadvantage, they are generally seen as unfair. Yet it is not this simple.

First, it is not just a matter of "whites versus blacks." Research shows a similar pattern with many disadvantaged ethnic groups. Aboriginal Australians tend to score lower than all other Australians.[15] Turkish and Surinamese immigrants in the Netherlands tend to score lower than Dutch test takers.[16] And Moroccan immigrants in Belgium tend to score lower than other Belgians.[17] Moreover, whites are not the racial group that scores highest of all. Rather, it is East Asians.

What complicates the situation and makes it contentious is not that intelligence tests do not work for some ethnic subgroups. They work fine: in fact, the ability of these tests to predict performance is roughly the same for all ethnic groups.[18] So even among ethnic groups that tend on average to do poorly on intelligence tests, individuals' test scores are still good predictors of whether they will succeed. And in this respect, for businesses that just want the people most likely to perform well—regardless of race—they appear fair tests of talent.

Looming over this issue are some huge ethical and societal concerns. Discrimination, social equality, and meritocracy are all mentioned in the debate over intelligence tests. Some argue that intelligence tests perpetuate societal inequalities. Others think that not using them or engaging in positive discrimination is not meritocratic. Whole books have been written on the subject. Yet for many businesses, the debate is not so much about ethics as about the practical issue of diversity: the desire to have a diverse talent pool and recruit from all population groups.

There is no easy solution. You may see some vendors suggesting that they have "culture-free" intelligence tests that do not result in any adverse impact. Do not believe them, because there is no such thing. We often, for example, hear an otherwise excellent intelligence test called Raven's Matrices referred to as "culture free." But the research is clear: like all other intelligence tests, it can result in adverse impact.[19] Indeed, we know of no measurement method that has been independently proven to be as powerful and yet free from adverse impact. In fact, we know of no other method at all that is free from it. Intelligence tests have made all the headlines because of the amount of adverse impact involved and the sheer volume of research into the matter. But interviews, situational judgment tests, assessment centers, résumé reviewing, and work sample tests have all been shown to be vulnerable to creating adverse impact.[20]

Businesses thus seem to be faced with two stark choices.[21] They can either sacrifice validity by using measures that are less

Legality and Diversity: Recommendations

1. *Be clear on your legal obligations.* In foreign locations, this is best achieved through local HR leaders or local vendors.

2. *Check the potential adverse impact of tools.* The easiest way to do this is to ask vendors for evidence of the adverse impact associated with their tools. And be specific: ask about national differences and the average scores for each ethnic group. Do not merely be satisfied with average scores for whites and nonwhites. These broad comparisons can hide differences that exist for more specific groups. Finally, beware of statements such as, "The test does not show any ethnic differences beyond those already reported in research." This just means that the test has all the adverse impact of any other test.[22]

3. *To reduce adverse impact, use a range of methods.* For example, combining an SJT or personality test with an intelligence measure can reduce adverse impact while adding incremental validity.[23]

4. *If diversity is important for your business, conduct regular adverse impact studies.* These are quick and easy and help you to ensure that the measurement methods you are using are enabling you to identify a diverse group of talent. Once a year, compare the demographics of everyone you assess with measurement processes with the people you eventually select or identify as desired talent. If they are broadly the same, then you do not have significant amounts of adverse impact.

valid than intelligence tests but do not result in as much adverse impact. Or they can sacrifice diversity by ignoring the potential adverse impact of intelligence tests. So what should you do?

Finding a Way Forward.   Organizations in countries like the United States and South Africa have had to act: the law gives them little option. Many businesses outside these countries, though, simply ignore the issue. This certainly is an easy route, and for some businesses operating in ethnically homogeneous areas, it is fine. But for businesses operating in more racially mixed areas or across national boundaries, such a policy cannot be recommended.

Awareness of this has led some organizations to stop using intelligence tests altogether. Yet a number of studies have highlighted how stopping using them can lead to a decrease in the quality of those hired. Moreover, by stopping measuring intelligence and assessing only other things, you can inadvertently replace one form of adverse impact with another. For example, research has shown that selecting people only on the basis of personality scores can lead to adverse impact against women.[24]

Another commonly suggested solution is banding: grouping scores into broad bands, such as high, medium, and low. The idea is that it can reduce adverse impact by making the bands so broad that they include people from ethnic groups who generally score lower. The efficacy of banding, however, has been hotly debated. In our opinion, it can help, but you are still left with the question of how to select people from within bands, so it is not a complete solution.

An additional possible solution has come from research showing that confidence can improve test performance, whereas anxiety can reduce it. The idea is that minority groups know that they tend to do less well on these tests, which makes them anxious and so reduces how well they do. And research has indeed shown that when the evaluation element of a test is downplayed, the performance of minority groups increases and adverse impact is reduced.[25] Yet the research is also clear that although doing this may reduce adverse impact a little, substantial group differences remain.[26]

Of course, so far all that we have really touched on is the example of intelligence and ethnicity. There are other forms of adverse impact as well. In many countries, discrimination on the basis of disability, gender, or age is illegal. Avoiding adverse impact against disability tends to be more of an implementation issue, and we return to this in chapter 6. The impact of various measurement methods on gender is well researched. Differences between the performance of men and women on both intelligence and personality tests do exist, but they vary considerably among tests. In terms of age, there is evidence that performance on intelligence tests reduces with age, in particular on tests that require many questions to be answered in a short time.[27] There is also research showing that people become less extraverted and agreeable with age.[28] The impact of age on talent measures, however, is an evolving field, and businesses have generally not yet shown much interest in it.

So legal issues can mean a whole heap of trouble for businesses, but with forethought and care, you can avoid them.

How Well a Method Is Likely to Work

No business wants to spend time and money on a measurement method that does not work. This is why most businesses know to ask this basic question: "How valid is this method or test?" The challenge only begins here, though, because you then need to be able to understand and evaluate the answer. To help you, try following these seven tactics.

Ask for Evidence. We were recently looking at the validity of a popular US interviewing system that described itself as being accurate and valid. On a Web page entitled "Validity," the vendor described a wide variety of research showing that interviews can be valid predictors of success. Yet there was not a single mention of any research that the vendor had conducted into the validity of its own system. So rule number one is that you need to get specific and ask vendors for the evidence that their particular method or tool is valid. And beware of statements such as, "The test is predictive," but do not come with any specific validity figures or evidence.

Ask What Is Meant by Validity. Validity figures are not always what they appear to be. For starters, there is no one way for vendors to measure or report validity. When you are told that a measurement method has 80 percent validity, it could mean many different things. Classically, *validity* refers to whether the ratings and scores that people achieve on particular measures can predict their performance in a business. And by and large, this is what you should expect to hear. Yet we have seen some vendors define validity as being whether individuals agree with the results, so when a vendor tells you that a particular measure is valid, you need to ask, "In what way?"

In response to this question, you may sometimes hear phrases such as "content validity," "criterion validity," and "construct validity." If you want to know more about what each of these means, check out the validity section in the appendix at the end of this book. For many people, though, this kind of technical jargon can be confusing and can put them off from delving more deeply into the subject. But it need not do so. All you need to remember is that you are essentially trying to find out two things: "How do you know that the method or tool measures what it is supposed to?" and, "What business outcomes do results with this method predict, and to what degree?"

It is worth noting here that "performance" can mean different things. It can mean actual results (such as sales figures), managers' appraisal ratings of individuals, and even self-ratings of performance. Beyond task performance, it can mean contribution to team performance or organizational citizenship behavior.

Furthermore, just because a measure can predict performance in skilled and semiskilled workers does not mean that it can also predict performance in managers. There are additional questions that you need to ask when told that a measure can predict performance: "What types of performance?" and, "In what types of people?" Moreover, with measures of potential, extra questions to ask are, "How far ahead can it predict performance?" and, "After how long?"

Beyond Validity

In this book we mainly focus on validity as a key indicator of whether a particular measure or method is effective. There is actually a lot more to determining whether measures are effective than just validity—things like alpha coefficients and scale intervals. We have deliberately chosen not to go into these because they are for the most part deeply technical issues that cannot be lightly touched on, and in our experience, most business users of measurement have neither the time nor need to commit to a full understanding of them. For most businesspeople, then, focusing on issues such as validity and reliability is enough. That does not mean that you shouldn't delve deeper, however. Should you want to, you will find in the appendix further details about validity and information on where you can learn about some of the more technical issues.

Beware of Very High Validity Figures. When looking at the degree to which methods or tools can predict outcomes, remember that the single best predictor of performance, intelligence, can achieve maximum validities of only 0.5 to 0.6. If you hear anything more than that, start asking questions.

Check How Many People the Tool Has Been Validated With. One essential question to ask is, "How many people?" For instance, if you are told that a measure can predict, say, absenteeism in semiskilled workers, you need to ask how many people were tested. If the answer comes back with anything fewer than one hundred, then the results may not be reliable. For psychometric tests, ideally you should be looking for two thousand or more people to have been tested.

If the Method or Tool Uses Norm Groups, Check the Quality and Relevance of Them. Not all methods and tools use norm groups, but some rely on them. Norm groups are comparison groups, a kind of benchmark. They enable you to compare the score of a particular individual on a certain test or measurement method with the scores of other people who have also done the test. This is particularly useful with ability tests, such as measures of intelligence and physical fitness, as it can help you understand what scores mean. For example, an individual may get a score of 25 out of 30 on an intelligence test, which sounds good. But if you then find out that the average score is 27, that score of 25 does not look so good after all. We need to know how well others usually perform to understand precisely how good a score is.

As useful as norm groups may sound, the science of developing them and where they should and should not be used are much-debated issues. What is important for our purposes here is simply that if you are going to use norm groups, then it is critical that they be good ones: if they are not, they may be misleading.

So what counts as a "good" norm group? You need to look for two qualities.[29] The first is size—the number of people in the group. Simply put, the bigger, the better. With competency ratings from individual psychological assessments, the norm group may be very small—under one hundred. For psychometrics, however, it will ideally be in the thousands.

The second quality you should look for is relevance. Having a norm group of two thousand white males from Scandinavia is impressive, but if you are trying to interpret the scores of Singaporean women, it is of no use. To be effective, then, a norm group needs to be representative of the people you are assessing. This can be in terms of gender, age, ethnicity, and education level. It can also be in terms of industry, function, and type of role. The more relevant, the better. For job applicants being tested with an intelligence test, for example, the best norm group is not the scores of people already employed, but other applicants for the same type of roles.

One quick way to evaluate the quality of a norm group you are already using is to look at how many of the people you are assessing score above the average for the norm group. If the norm group is perfect, then 50 percent of your people will score above the norm average and 50 percent will score below it. If almost everyone is scoring above or below the norm average, then you know that the norm group may not be relevant enough.

Moreover, for larger organizations it may be worthwhile trying to create your own norm groups specific to your business. The absolute minimum you need for competency and individual psychological assessment ratings is around 50 people. This is low, though, and you would need to be a little cautious about comparisons. For psychometrics, the minimum is around 150 people, although once again this is low. A number you could be completely confident in would be around 2,000, so our suggestions are absolute minimums. Some vendors will try to charge you for creating a specific norm group for your business. Others do not charge. Obviously, we recommend the latter.

Remember Reliability. For relatively objective methods such as psychometric tests and SJTs, you do not need to ask about reliability. A test cannot be valid without also being reliable, so asking about validity is enough. However, for more subjective methods such as assessment centers and individual psychological assessment, it is important to ask about interrater reliability. This is the degree to which two assessors agree (or disagree) in their ratings and judgments about people. The less reliability and agreement there is between assessors, the less likely results are to be accurate.

Look for Independent Reviews. This final step is an important one: always look for independent evidence of whether measures work. An easy place to start here is to ask the vendor if any such research exists. You can also do a Web search for the name of the tool. Moreover, with psychometric tests, probably the best thing you can do is to check one of the independent, nonprofit bodies that publish test reviews. The national psychology associations or societies of many countries provide this kind of service. By far our favorite is provided by the University of Nebraska's Buros Institute. Its reviews can contain some deeply technical information, but they also contain some clear and no-nonsense recommendations on whether to use tests.

These, of course, are just questions about validity. However, as we argued in chapter 3, businesses need to think more broadly about the issue of whether measures work. We have discussed, for example, the need to ask about incremental validity. Yet businesses also need to think about what measures need to do over and above merely predicting performance. This could include things like helping managers engage potential new employees, identifying areas new employees may need support with, and helping plan for individuals' development. Validity, then, is not the be-all and end-all, and the most valid test is sometimes not the one that will work best for your business. Nevertheless, it is a good place to start: a test that is not valid will not be able to do much for your business.

Whether the Method Works: Recommendations

1. *Think broadly about what measurement methods need to do.* Think about what they need to achieve over and above measuring particular things and predicting performance.

2. *Do not just accept vendors' validity statements.* Question them intensely.

3. *Check for independent reviews of tests.* An example is the Buros Institute.

4. *For more subjective methods, ask about interrater reliability.* This particularly applies to assessment centers and individual psychological assessments. Ask to see the details of studies that vendors have undertaken on this.

How Much a Method Costs and How Long It Takes

These two issues are both fairly straightforward and are without doubt the two most common questions we hear managers ask when choosing measurement methods.

With cost, the challenge is to identify what the total cost will be. This is not always simple because of the need to factor in not only immediate defined costs but also potential future costs. Some of these can be obvious, such as initial setup fees, facilities required, and ongoing project management. Others can be less apparent, like the need to develop alternative versions of recruitment situational judgment tests (so that leaked information about how to "pass" them does not enable people to cheat) or the need to develop translations of psychometrics for all the nationalities you need to cover. We return to some of these less obvious issues when we look at contracting with vendors in chapter 8.

For now, two principles are important. First, businesses need to have a clear and definitive costing. And second, when it comes to measurement, lower cost rarely means better. With online psychometrics, for example, if you find a tool priced below the market average, it is likely to be below average quality too. Similarly, driving down the cost of individual psychological assessment can be self-defeating if taken too far, as vendors tend to use less experienced and expensive assessors. And as we have seen, the quality of assessors is all-important.

As for how long a method will take, it is important to know the development time: how long it will take to develop and set up the measurement method. In addition, a bigger worry for frontline managers is the fear that adding measurement to a recruitment process could cause them to lose candidates by making the process take too long. We understand this concern and know that slow processes can lead to lost candidates. In fact, a recent study found that one in three UK firms reports that the length of its recruitment process has led to the loss of potential recruits.[30] Yet many methods are very time efficient. Indeed, in our experience, the addition of a measurement process is rarely the reason that companies lose candidates. Instead, where time is an issue, it is often the time that other elements of the recruitment process take.

Of course, time and money often boil down to the same thing. As we reported in chapter 4, developmental assessment centers are becoming shorter in an effort to save time-out-of-business costs. One method where the overlap of time and money can be less obvious, though, is 360-degree feedback. In our experience, firms often do not take into account the cost of people taking time to give feedback. As a guide, each rating question takes about six seconds on average to answer, and each word of written feedback takes about eight seconds. These seconds can add up. Indeed, it is common for 360s to take fifteen to twenty minutes or more to complete. Moreover, each participant typically nominates between six and eight feedback givers. So it is easy for the total time taken by all of them to give their feedback to be over two and half hours. This may not sound a lot for one individual, but once you start to multiply it by the total number of 360s you are doing, it can add up to a surprisingly large amount. Undoubtedly, 360-degree feedback can be a highly cost-effective method. But it needs to be done right.

Cost and Time: Recommendations

1. *Make sure you are clear on potential costs as well as immediate actual costs.* If you are asking multiple vendors to submit proposals (which you should be), cross-referencing what each vendor has itemized can help reveal hidden or optional costs.

2. *Calculate time-out-of-business costs.* These can involve more than just the test taker, and although the costs may not be that significant for each case, the total can mount up.

3. *Do not just buy cheap.* It rarely pays.

Making the Choice

In this chapter, we have discussed various situational and company-specific factors to weigh as you choose methods for measuring talent. We have looked at location; what you choose to measure, and why; legality and diversity; likelihood of success; and costs in time and money. For individual businesses, there may well be other issues, but for most, answering these questions will enable you to choose which tool to use.

These, of course, are just the broad issues, and they often need to be followed by more specific questions, such as which vendor to use, which personality test to use, or the capabilities of a particular 360-degree feedback tool. Unfortunately, we cannot answer this more specific type of question for you because it depends on your circumstances. But in the appendix at the back of this book, we do offer some pointers to help you make these more specific decisions.

Up to now, we have looked at how to identify talent—at the indicators of it that can be measured, the methods of measurement, and how to choose among them. Yet choosing the right measures and tools is only the start. If they are not implemented and used effectively, even the best tools have little impact. And in our experience, implementation—actually doing ongoing talent measurement in your company—is where the real challenges lie.

Over the next three chapters, we therefore look at how to implement talent measurement. To be clear here, we are not talking about operational issues such as how to run assessment centers or project-manage a large-scale assessment process, but broader implementation issues. In chapter 6, we explore the foundations that need to be in place for talent measurement to work effectively, such as competency frameworks, databases, and policy issues. In chapter 7, we look at what you need to do to ensure that measurement methods and tools are used to best effect and how to make the most of the data they provide. And finally, in chapter 8, we look at how to source the expertise to do these things and how to choose and manage measurement vendors.

Using New Technology to Do More Than Just Measure

CASE STUDY

Online technologies are enabling measurement vendors to do some interesting new things, including fulfilling some of the nonassessment aspects of measurement. Consider the collaboration between one of the UK's best-known pharmacy-led retailers and the global measurement vendor Cubiks.

To support its ambition of providing excellent customer care, the retailer decided to develop a new recruitment process specifically designed to identify the candidates best able to deliver this customer experience. As part of the process, it asked Cubiks to develop a new online measurement tool that could help it efficiently and effectively short-list the best candidates from an estimated 1 million applications per year.

The tool obviously had to involve a robust assessment and be a strong predictor of performance. But it also needed to do more: it had to provide a highly engaging experience for candidates, support the company's brand, and present a detailed preview of the role so candidates has realistic expectations of it.

The tool took months to build, but it was worth the wait. Applicants are first shown around a store and presented with typical workplace scenarios. They are then "interviewed" by a virtual store manager, which asks them questions about how they typically behave in work settings. This interview is in fact a cleverly disguised personality test, which produces both some detailed results about candidates' personalities and an overall "fit" score to assist the shortlisting process.

Initial feedback from both candidates and hiring managers has been excellent, and the tool has won a number of industry awards. Candidates like it because it gives them a good sense of what working for the company is like. The business likes it because it communicates the company's brand values while making the hiring process both quicker and more effective.

It is too early to tell how predictive the test is. But the time taken to hire people has been significantly reduced, since fewer candidates are short-listed, and those who are appear to be of a higher caliber than in the past.

6

BUILDING THE FOUNDATIONS FOR TALENT MEASUREMENT

For some readers, the suggestion of a chapter dealing with foundations, infrastructure, and—dare we even say it—policy may sound dreadfully dull. But as we hope that we will show it is anything but dull. Indeed, getting these issues right is possibly the single biggest opportunity that firms have to maximize the impact and value of talent measurement. This is because what these issues tend to affect most is what you can do with the outputs and results of measurement. And even the best tools are only as valuable as what you can do with the results. Consequently, these seemingly fringe tasks are in fact a critical part of the measurement process. Not done right, they are one of the main reasons talent measurement can fail to have the impact it should. Done well, they are the key to turning talent data into genuine talent intelligence.

In this chapter, then, we explore the foundations that talent measurement needs to be built on in order to be effective—the elements that need to be in place around it for measurement to have the impact it should. We look first at four essential foundations that you absolutely must have in place: central data collection, common data points, a check on whether measures work, and processes to ensure proper use. We then look at the strategic and policy issues that you need to be aware of and consider but may not always have to act on. And finally, we introduce one further foundation—the measurement of different types of performance—that has the potential to radically improve the quality of measures and tools available to organizations.

There are some easy wins here too—some low-hanging fruit that every organization using measurement can take advantage of. The challenge is mostly just knowing what they are.

Why Foundations Are Often Missing

Many of the foundations for measurement we discuss in this chapter may sound obvious, yet they are often overlooked. This is partly because they are less visible than the more upfront challenges of choosing which measure to use. It is also because they require some strategic planning, something that the use of measurement processes does not often include.

In most companies, measurement use is usually driven by practical operational issues as they arise. A small business may elect to use measurement in one particular recruitment process, or a particular business unit within a larger organization may decide it wants to assess people as part of a change project. Either way, talent measurement often has small beginnings and then spreads from there.

This demand-driven approach is certainly practical, but it tends to leave broader issues largely unaddressed. As a result, the foundations required for effective measurement are often not in place. A classic sign of this is when the implementation of talent measurement varies considerably in different parts of a business. Unfortunately, in our work with organizations, we have found that an ad hoc approach is the norm in most businesses, and there are several major risks associated with it:

- *Measurement processes are more likely to vary in quality,* reducing their impact on the business.
- *Measurement outputs (the results) may be employed in ways that limit their value.* Assessment reports, for example, may not be used properly or may not be linked to other processes such as onboarding or training.

- *There may be no central collection of results.* This prevents firms from pooling and comparing data from different processes or parts of the organization.
- *Different competency frameworks may be used.* Again, this can prevent data from being pooled and can limit the degree to which businesses can build benchmarks.
- *Policies regarding digital security and data protection, for example, may vary or be missing.* This can create regulatory compliance and litigation risks.
- *Assessment vendors tend to be managed locally,* resulting in mixed quality and missed financial opportunities for economies of scale.
- *There is likely to be no central oversight of the total spending on measurement.* In one business we worked with, for instance, we found that the business units were spending over $25 million between them. Yet because of the siloed nature of the firm, it had no idea that it was spending this much overall.

Thus, even organizations that make limited use of talent measurement need to be aware of the broader foundational challenges because they cannot be overcome by leaving them to chance. Foundations need to be designed, and the earlier they are in place, the sooner organizations can start making sure that measurement processes have the impact that they should.

So what are these issues? To help us think about this, we like to distinguish between two kinds of foundational issues: the things that organizations absolutely must do to guarantee impact and value from talent measurement and the things that they need to be aware of and think about but do not necessarily need to act on. We look at each of these in turn.

Four Things You Must Do to Make Measurement Work

Every company must put four core foundations in place to make measurement work:

- Collect data centrally.
- Use common data points.
- Check the impact of measures.
- Ensure proper use.

Collect Data Centrally

The first building block for effective measurement is to collect data centrally. All assessment results should be gathered in one place. Interview ratings, psychometric scores, competency ratings: all need to be collated from throughout the business. Wherever measurement data exist, they need to be drawn in. It may be possible to use an HR information technology system to store the data, but at the very least, there needs to be a large, central spreadsheet containing all results and a secure place to keep all reports. The centrality of the database is critical too, so that the data can be shared. In businesses with both recruitment and learning teams, for example, it should sit outside both so it is not viewed as belonging to one, but not the other.

Without centrally collecting talent data, businesses cannot build up a picture of the talent across the organization. Instead, all they will have are fragments of information relating only to individuals or teams. Not collecting measurement data is like buying a sports car and then leaving it on the driveway or using it only to drive the kids to school. You will only ever enjoy a small margin of the value that the car can provide.

Even when firms do not use measurement methods much, they should still collect the data so that they can follow trends over time. In some firms, for example, measurement is limited to recruitment interviews, and the only outputs are a whether-to-hire rating and perhaps competency ratings. These may not seem like much, but they can be extremely useful and ought to be collected. Data are only as useful as the insights they give, and the insights they give are vastly increased when they are connected with other data.

For example, knowing the average competency ratings of newly hired employees can be useful. Yet if you also know the performance scores of the newly hired one year after they have joined the business, you can see which competencies are most predictive of initial success. If you know who is still employed three years later, you can work out which factors are most predictive of retention. And knowing who is later promoted can provide insight into the types of talent valued in your business and the qualities predictive of longer-term success.

Moreover, because companies need not only to gather talent data, but also to join those data with other information, they should never be tempted to let a vendor take care of data collection for them. Businesses must own and control their measurement data, because only they can connect these results to other talent data. Right from the start, they need to record other relevant talent data alongside the measurement results—things like performance scores, promotion dates, business unit, location, and key demographic data. And it is critical to do this from the very beginning because the fragmented nature of many larger companies' systems and processes can make gathering this information extremely challenging in retrospect.

We look in more detail at what organizations can do with measurement data in the next chapter. For now, the key point is that if measurement results are to be useful for more than merely informing individual people decisions, data need to be collected centrally. They are valuable resources and should be managed as such.

Use Common Data Points

Just collecting talent measurement data centrally is not enough, however. For this information to be meaningful and useful, you need to have common data points. For example, if you measure one person's intelligence and another's personality, bringing the two pieces of information together will not tell you much. But if you know the personalities of both people, then you can compare them. And if you know this for enough people, you can compare individuals to the average profiles of a group or the qualities of different groups, such as the leadership teams of different business units. It is therefore critical that as far as possible, you know the same information about different employees. Without this, any measurement database will be of little value in what it can tell you, and talent analytics will simply not be possible.

One significant step in this direction can be to ensure that if you use intelligence or personality tests in your business, you use the same tests and not different ones from different vendors. This is important because comparing the scores from two different tests can be very difficult and is often impossible. Using the same tests is not always easy to achieve, though, since business or HR leaders often have their own favorite tools. And for large multinationals, it may not be completely possible: they may find, for instance, that the intelligence test that most suits the majority of the business is not available in some locations. Yet as far as possible, the guiding principle ought to be that the tools and tests you use should be standardized.

In many businesses, the main tools used to measure talent are competency frameworks. These describe the skills, behaviors, and attributes that individuals are thought to need to be successful. They can exist for single job families, but can also be used to define the capabilities required in particular groups of people across whole business units or organizations. For example, many businesses have a set of leadership competencies that are used for all of their senior leaders or technical competencies specific to particular functions. As a result, competency frameworks provide an excellent opportunity for ensuring there are common data points.

There is a tension here, however. On the one hand, the fewer frameworks your business has, the more able it will be to collate and compare competency ratings from different parts of the business. Yet on the other hand, as we saw in chapter 3, when assessments take into account the specific circumstances and needs of a business unit or team, then those assessments are likely to be more accurate in predicting individuals' success in those environments. So the more specific and personal that a competency framework is to your company or business unit, the more effective it is likely to be for measuring talent. And if we follow this line of reasoning, then larger businesses may well be better off with lots of different frameworks, each specific to a particular part of the organization.

So although a single common framework is probably appropriate for small firms, a compromise is required for large or diversified businesses. They need both business-specific frameworks that enable an accurate evaluation of the fit between individuals and business needs and common data points in order to be able to use the measurement data for more than just informing individual people decisions.

The solution here is compromise. The guiding principle should always be to have as few frameworks as possible, so that there are some common data points between people of different levels and in different parts of the business. Yet this still leaves room for competencies specific to particular populations. One approach that we have seen work well is to have both generic and business unit–specific behavioral competencies, in addition to technical ones. This allows both common data points and tailored, business-specific assessments. For example, a company could have a framework that consists of:

- Technical competencies specific to particular functions or job families. In small firms, this could be a single competency called "technical knowledge." In organizations with significantly sized functions, there could be a collection of competencies for each technical area.

- Two or three behavioral competencies specific to each of its business units that describe what is required to succeed in each area.

- Three or four generic behavioral competencies against which everyone is evaluated. If some abilities are specific to the leadership populations, then an additional one or two can be added for this group.

As an example of this approach, consider a large, global energy firm we worked with. It had a competency framework that it used across the whole firm to collect common data points. One business unit, though, decided to supplement this with three additional competencies. It believed that these more accurately described the necessary qualities to succeed in its particular business area. Two years later, it was proved correct. The three unit-specific competencies more accurately predicted performance than the wider firm's generic framework.[1]

One final point to note here is that not just any competencies will do: they need to be suitable for measurement (and not all of them are). Developing effective competency frameworks is a subject worthy of a book in its own right. Because our focus here is the need for common data points rather than competencies, we will not dwell further on their construction at this time. However, in the appendix at the back of this book, we address the issue of how you can tell whether a framework is suitable for measuring talent.

Collecting common data points is thus an essential foundation for obtaining meaningful data. Like collecting data centrally, it is an absolute must for organizations hoping to build up a picture of the talent across the business.

Check the Impact of Measures

The third must-do action for businesses in making measurement effective is to check whether the methods and tools they use work. All too often, companies see that a tool has a certain validity and then seem to take it for granted that it will have the desired impact. In this respect, when it comes to measurement, organizations appear to be running on faith. A recent survey showed that 79 percent believe that measurement adds value to their organization, but only 23 percent actually check that it does.[2]

Why is checking impact so important? One obvious reason is that spending money on a service without having any idea if it works is plainly bad business. A less obvious one is that measurement methods are not like most other products that you buy. Despite what some vendors may try to tell you, most of the time most tools do not reach you as finished products. If you are using psychometric tests with a limited number of people, then there is little, if any, finishing to do, and using them straight off the shelf is fine. But most methods require some extra tuning, especially if you are going to be using them a lot (for example, with over one hundred people). Norm groups need to be built, exercises adjusted, and tools tailored to measure fit with a particular organization, business unit, or role. None of this can happen without some feedback about whether the measure is in fact working.

We live in a world where most of the products and services we buy and use work perfectly the first time. We expect this, even demand it. But talent measures are precision instruments, and they require optimizing. You should not expect them to work perfectly straightaway. Indeed, when you first check their efficacy, you should expect to find room for improvement.

Nancy Tippins, a past president of the American Psychological Association's organizational psychology division, has spoken passionately about this. As she puts it, "Businesses often buy a measurement product and then do not do anything else with it. They expect it to work straight out of the box. To get the most from these products, though, they need to continually hone and optimize them."[3] Evaluating impact is important not only for checking if measures work, but also for making them work.

Some companies require vendors to check these issues for them. But no matter how positive your relationship with a vendor is, asking it to evaluate its own tools is not advisable. There is just too much vested interest. By all means, ask a vendor to help share the work involved, but you must own and lead your own process.

Moreover, we are not simply talking about checking and honing the efficacy of a vendor's products. Evaluating impact is also vital to help managers improve their people decisions. For example, one business we work with always follows up the "failure" of new employees with a review meeting involving the hiring manager or recruitment lead. The meeting usually lasts no more than thirty minutes. During it, the information available at the time of hiring is reviewed to see if any potential signs of failure were missed. The idea is not to lay blame, but to have a genuinely curious inquiry with the aim of helping people improve their selection skills.

So how can businesses go about evaluating impact? There are two main ways. There are simple validity studies, which check whether ratings or results predict subsequent performance, and there are impact studies. For promotion decisions, an example of an impact study would be following up to check success rates among those promoted. For recruitment decisions, meanwhile, quality of hire metrics can be used. These include a variety of indicators. The trick is not to track them all, but to select and focus on just a few. Monitoring these indicators need not be complicated, either. In fact if you have the first two foundations in place—centrally collected data and common data points— then it can be quick and easy to check the data regularly. The list of possibilities is long and includes the following:

- Retention figures
- Performance ratings
- Hiring manager's satisfaction with new employees
- New employees' reactions to the measurement process
- New employees' end-of-year bonus allocation
- Comparison of competency ratings at hiring interview and at first annual appraisal
- Whether a new employee is tagged as high potential within an agreed time period
- The number of legal challenges to a selection process

So our third foundation is the need to check whether measures work and their impact on actual people decisions—not as some kind of after-the-fact evaluation but as an integral part of making measurement work.

Ensure Proper Use

The first three foundations are all fairly simple. They do not take significant time or resources. All they really need is a little will. The final foundation can be a bit tougher. It is the need to ensure that the tools and methods of measurement are used properly. You can have the best tests in the world, but if you do not use them properly, they are not going to work as well as they should.

There are two issues here. The first is making sure that tools are used for proper and appropriate purposes. For example, some types of personality psychometrics—called ipsative tests—are suitable only for development processes, not selection (see the appendix). Some types of tools do not work with particular populations. English-language intelligence tests, for instance, should be used only with people for whom English is their mother tongue. And some types of tools should probably never be used, such as Facebook content and credit scores.

The second issue is making sure that the outputs of measurement processes—the ratings, results, and reports—are used properly. For example, you can make sure that managers do not hire only one personality type or that hiring decisions do indeed take measurement results into account. We have seen too many businesses that have put great effort into identifying the best tools to use, only to leave it to line managers to decide how they want to use them. And inevitably this leads to mixed or poor use of the outputs.

These two issues are usually easier for smaller companies than larger ones. In decentralized businesses, they can be particularly challenging. Nonetheless, organizations need to do something, and they have two basic options:

- *Mandate particular measurement processes.* For example, many firms stipulate that some people decisions, such as hiring above a certain level of seniority, are supported by the use of particular measures. Others insist on involving people who have attended specific training (such as advanced interviewing skills).

- *Guide use.* Some organizations provide lists of recommended tools and vendors to ensure overall consistency while still allowing business units some flexibility in their choices.

The route businesses choose will depend on their size and culture. What makes ensuring proper use so challenging for some businesses is the fact that it requires consistency. For larger, decentralized, or geographically dispersed organizations, this can be tough. Moreover, it touches on the activity and decisions of individual managers and leaders, which can be quite politically sensitive in some firms. And, of course, the key to being able to ensure proper use is having access to expertise, which many companies do not.

Yet despite the difficulties, businesses need to act to ensure that measurement outputs are used properly and to best effect. We return to this topic in the next chapter. For the moment, though, what is important is to acknowledge that it is a crucial issue and one that must not be ignored.

Two Things You Need to Think About

In addition to these four foundations that organizations absolutely must lay to make measurement work, there are, of course, other issues they need to be aware of and think about. These issues may not be as fundamental, but they are important. Some of them can have a significant impact on the efficacy of measurement. Others are levers that businesses can use to ensure proper use. We like to divide these issues into two camps: strategy and policy.

Strategy

As we have noted, the development of measurement practices in most businesses is not a strategic affair. It is emergent and demand led, and by and large, this is fine. In fact, it is essential that measurement processes serve a real business need.

The closest most businesses get to having a measurement strategy is when they consider one of three main issues: whom to assess, centralization, and standardization. Yet as we will go on to show, there is a fourth issue as well; it is rarely raised but has the potential to be the most strategic one of all.

Whom to Assess. It is rare for businesses to think about this early on, before they assess anyone. But the question often comes up when they are thinking about expanding a particular measurement process—for example, whether to expand the use of individual psychological assessments from only executives to the wider senior management population.

In our experience, rather than thinking about which groups of people to assess, businesses are better off thinking about the talent issues they want to address. They can then target measurement processes to support these. To deal with the question of whether to expand individual psychological assessment to senior leaders, then, we would check the quality and success rates of recently hired senior management. If all looks good, there may be no imperative to expand the use of these assessments.

The ROI of Measurement

To help you think about whom to assess, there are four scenarios in particular in which measurement, done well, can deliver a substantial return:

- When a large volume of candidates needs to be sifted
- When significant cost is associated with selection failure—for example, where there is a high risk of accidents or in senior executive assessment
- When there is a significant need for perceived fairness or objectivity—for instance, during a restructuring or in countries with heavy regulatory requirements
- When input is required on where best to target learning and development—for example, when deciding which people to offer training to or when trying to identify what specific individuals' development needs are

---

Centralization and Standardization. These second and third strategy issues are often seen as the same, but in fact whether to centralize and whether to standardize measurement processes across the business are separate questions. *Centralization* is mainly about positioning in the business. It is about reporting lines and whether decision-making authority lies at the center of the business or within individual business units. *Standardization*, by contrast, is about aligning processes. We mentioned earlier, for example, that some organizations use the same tools or vendors across their business to help ensure common data points. So you can have centralization without aligning any processes and you can have standardization without having decision-making authority.

Companies often try to pursue centralization and standardization because of the benefits they can bring. These include reduced costs through economies of scale, minimized duplication of effort, and better quality control. Indeed, they are the key mechanisms that firms have to ensure the proper use of tools. Yet they come at a cost. Most notable, they involve a trade-off with being able to adapt to and support the unique needs of different business units.

This is true for any process, but talent measurement has an added dimension because fully standardized measurement processes are not possible in global businesses due to the different legal and cultural contexts. What you are allowed to do with data can vary among countries. Measures often have to be adapted to local use, and locally developed measures may need to be used in some cases. The question is not so much whether to centralize or standardize, but what to centralize or standardize and what not to.

We have already mentioned the need to centralize data collection and standardize certain data points. There are other options too. The most common way to centralize measurement is through structure and reporting lines, with a central point of expertise or oversight for measurement. Another common option is to have a centrally set preferred supplier list. We explore both of these options in more detail in chapter 8.

Organizations also often centralize through funding. For example, the cost of measurement processes can be paid by each business unit or can come out of a central budget. The advantage of local payment is that leaders are more likely to value something that they pay for themselves. The advantage of central payment is that it can be a better way to ensure that leaders do use a measurement process. There is no one right way of doing this, and the broader business culture and structure will usually determine which is pursued.

As for standardization, this commonly involves ensuring that similar products and processes are used across the business. Companies are also increasingly adapting the outputs of different tools so they all look similar, even though they may come from different vendors. This can help ensure that methods and tools feel familiar to managers and do not require extra training. Finally, standardization also includes ensuring that outputs are used consistently, a topic we look at in more detail in the next chapter.

A Fourth Strategic Conversation. This issue is not often raised, but it is the most strategic of the lot. It is *how to use measurement to identify, support, and solve the talent issues that businesses face.*

In our experience, businesses tend to use measurement processes to support individual decisions, but do not think further than this. We came across a business, for example, that had been using formal measurement methods for five years. In that time, it had assessed thousands of people. And it had done almost everything right: it had collected data centrally, used common data points, worked to ensure proper use, and had even evaluated the impact of measures.

Yet what it had not done was to think about what it wanted to use measurement for beyond merely supporting individual people decisions. It had not considered how it might use the data it collected to gain insight into the flow of talent through the business. As a result, when harder times came and budgets were cut, the measurement was stopped. It was seen as high quality but not high value. It was not anchored in the real talent issues of the organization, and there was no clearly communicated link between it and business priorities.

To make measurement strategic and extract the maximum value from it, organizations need to think about what they want to use measurement for, above and beyond just measuring people. And in our experience, this conversation does not happen often enough.

Policy

As words go, *policy* hardly instills excitement. It certainly lacks the appeal of its sexier sibling, *strategy*, but it is no less important for that. Done well, creating policy is about giving simple, succinct, and clear guidance about what to do in certain situations.

We should state now that we believe policy should be kept to a minimum, and we are not fans of long policy documents. Thick manuals that lie unread are of little use. Brief, specific statements of principle, however, can be useful. At the very least, you need to be aware of some of these issues and know your position on them.

We tend to distinguish between two types of policy: those that emerge, developing out of issues as you first encounter them, and those that it is best to think through before any issues emerge. Emerging policies can be things like whether to retest people who report problems completing online ability tests or how to respond to some disability matters, such as using intelligence tests with people who are dyslexic. With these issues, the vendor is usually best placed to advise on how to respond. Companies do not need to have a stance on them beforehand, but they do need to learn from them when they do occur.

The policy issues that should be thought through before using measurement mostly concern data privacy and protection—in other words, who has access to individuals' measurement results and how these results are kept secure. The laws of the countries in which firms operate determine what they have to do here. One thing worth noting, though, is that there are some big national differences.

For instance, the United States may be far stricter about adverse impact than other countries (see chapter 5), but the European Union (EU) is far stricter about data privacy. Specifically, the 1995 Directive on Data Protection by the European Commission states that personal data may be transferred to other countries only if the countries provide adequate data protection. And according to the EU, the United States does not, so a US business with a European office or using an EU-based vendor could be restricted from sending data from the EU to the United States. Fortunately, there are some easy solutions that vendors can use, but you need to be aware of the regulations and comply with them.

Even companies that operate only in one location need to think about data privacy. For example, they need to consider how they will store data and keep them secure (larger firms may have a digital security department with its own policies on this). They also need to think about who will have access to measurement results. These can be simple decisions, but decisions do need to be made.

Larger companies tend to have a legal department to help them navigate these matters. For smaller firms, the easiest option is often to ask vendors for guidance. Since regulations differ, we cannot offer any definitive advice here, but as general guidance, we always try to follow four simple rules:

- Keep data secure—for example, lock reports in a cabinet, or password-protect a spreadsheet containing results.
- Give access to as few people as possible.
- Keep only the data you need.
- Keep data only as long as you need them. Where possible, make them anonymous.

One final factor you should think through before embarking on measurement processes is whether to provide feedback about measurement results to participants. When the measurement is part of a development process, the answer will almost always be yes. But with recruitment processes, it is not always so easy. Some companies see it as an ethical obligation. Others avoid it for fear of the risk of litigation. Some provide information only to successful candidates. Some do different things at different levels. And the feedback given can involve anything from a simple pass-or-fail statement to a detailed report and coaching session.

Factors influencing your decision will be the litigation environment of where you are operating and issues such as the number and level of candidates. There is no correct answer here, but our general advice is to give some level of feedback wherever possible. If nothing else, research has shown that when done sensitively, it can improve candidates' perceptions of the selection process and thus the reputation of the company.[4] Furthermore, whatever level of feedback is given, candidates should always be advised beforehand what to expect.

The Final Foundation: Linking Measurement to Performance

So far, we have looked at four fundamental foundations that must be laid for talent measurement to work and briefly explored the strategy and policy issues that businesses need to consider when using measurement. There is one final foundational issue that we need to look at. This foundation is not strictly absolutely necessary for measurement to work or a matter of strategy or policy. But put in place, it can significantly improve the quality of measures and tools available to organizations and thereby also improve the decisions they make about people.

As we mentioned in chapter 3, one of the curious things about talent measurement is that generally, the past thirty years have not seen the development of measures that are substantially more predictive. Ask vendors why and what their biggest challenges are in developing and improving assessments, and their response is usually the same: a shake of the head, a deep sigh, and sometimes even a pained expression. This is followed, almost always, by a common complaint often referred to as the *criterion issue*.

Despite sounding like a great name for a spy thriller, it refers to something rather more mundane, albeit critical. In this context it is the simple question, "How do we know whether a particular measure is linked to workplace success?"

The traditional answer is to look at whether measures are linked to individuals' performance in the workplace—for example, if we think that height is a sign of talent, we can test whether people who are tall do in fact tend to achieve higher levels of performance than people who are shorter. This may sound straightforward, but a big problem lurks here: how we measure performance. So before we look at how we can use measures of performance to improve talent measurement, let's first look at what some of the problems with measuring performance are.

Problems in Measuring Performance

In some roles, performance can be measured through results, for example, sales figures. Yet in most roles, there are no such straightforward results that can be used. Even when there are, using hard results as an indicator of performance is not always as perfect as it sounds. In sales jobs, for instance, there is the issue of whether it is fair to compare people who operate in different areas. As a result, researchers and vendors have tended not to use real results, but rather managers' performance ratings of people. Again, this may sound like a good solution, but it is not, for three reasons: lack of performance data, inaccurate performance ratings, and the fact that performance ratings can reflect many things.

Lack of Performance Data. Researchers and vendors can often struggle to access performance ratings. We know, for example, of a FTSE 10 firm that has been using certain tests for its graduate recruitment for five years, but in this time, it had has not made performance data available to validate the measure. This issue is often less of a problem in the United States because of the legal necessity of proving validity. But elsewhere it is a big challenge. It often stems from the fact that due to system limitations, companies can struggle to access these data themselves and match them to test results. Yet it is also often an issue of will: they feel they have other priorities.

Inaccurate Performance Ratings. Even when we can access performance ratings, they are not perfect indicators of actual performance. Ratings obviously reveal something about performance.[5] Yet there is strong evidence that ratings do not reflect only performance. Managers typically give higher ratings to employees they like, and it is not unusual to find 80 percent or more of employees rated as "above average."

Some companies have tried to address this issue by introducing forced ranking systems in their performance management processes. These require managers to identify a certain proportion of their employees as high and low performers. For example, they may have to rate 20 percent of their people as high performers, 70 percent as average performers, and 10 percent as low performers. Yet although these systems do stop the wide-scale overrating of performance, research has shown that they are not long-term solutions and can become counterproductive after a time.[6]

The quality of performance ratings can be problematic for researchers and vendors because for every bit that the data are slightly inaccurate or skewed, they reduce vendors' ability to accurately target measures to predict performance. Rather than predicting genuine performance levels, the data end up predicting the overinflated or skewed performance ratings.

Performance Ratings Reflect Many Things. Finally, and perhaps most significant of all, is that researchers have mostly used just overall performance ratings—mainly because this is all that most companies measure. Yet researchers have found that overall performance ratings are not based only on task performance. There are other aspects of performance too, such as corporate citizenship and self-development, that all contribute to the overall performance rating. And, critically, many talent measures appear more able to predict these more specific elements of performance than overall performance.[7] So, for example, there is evidence that conscientiousness is a better predictor of corporate citizenship than of overall performance.[8]

There is more: it also appears that talent measures may be better predictors of some types of performance than others. Research by the US Army, for instance, has found that intelligence is better able to predict task performance (with validities of 0.65) than "effort and leadership" (validity 0.25), "physical fitness and military bearing" (0.20), and "personal discipline" (0.16). Similarly, personality measures were found to be more strongly related to the physical fitness and military bearing dimension of performance than to task performance.[9]

In chapter 2, we saw that using more specific personality dimensions could lead to higher validity levels. What we now find here is that trying to predict more specific types of performance also increases the accuracy of predictions. Being more precise seems to be the way to go.

Measuring Multiple Dimensions of Performance

For vendors to be able to develop better tests and more effectively target measures, businesses have to start measuring more than just overall performance. Indeed, if they want to be better able to predict success and thereby improve their people decisions, this is arguably just as important as the need to start measuring fit. The big issue, of course, is how to do it.

Managers have increasingly broad spans of control, which means they have to invest a significant amount of time in performance management. The tendency has thus been to try to simplify and accelerate the process for them. Indeed, we recently saw an article in which a company boasted of having an appraisal form that takes a mere seven seconds to complete.[10] Putting aside the issue of whether this is something to aspire to, the reality is that any suggestion of greater complexity in the performance management process is likely to evoke concern. We want to be clear here. What we are proposing need not, and should not, be either complex or time-consuming. It need not add much extra work, but it does have the potential to make the ratings far more meaningful.

In fact, there is already a move to do this, especially in the United States. Companies are increasingly looking to monitor and reward employee behaviors that are discretionary and beyond their formal job descriptions that add value to the organization. They are called different things, such as organizational citizenship behavior, prosocial organizational behavior, extra-role behavior, and contextual performance.[11] But they mostly refer to the same thing—typically behaviors that contribute to making the workplace a better or easier place to work. Researchers have developed some detailed definitions and complex measures to help assess these behaviors. But managerial ratings need not be detailed or complex. They just need to be good enough.

Another increasingly common practice is competency-based performance management. This involves distinguishing between the results people achieve and the way they go about achieving them. This *how* element is usually measured through competencies, and it often contributes to 10 or even 20 percent of the overall performance score. This is definitely a step in the right direction. But the way it is implemented means that the data are often not useful for developing better talent measures. Managers are typically asked to rate a large number of competencies (we know one firm in which they have to rate eleven), which means the accuracy of the individual ratings tends to be low. Or they simply give an overall score for "behaviors," which is too broad to be useful for our purposes here.

Measuring What You Value

The final foundation we are suggesting, then, is replacing the overall performance rating with three or four more specific ratings. The types of performance you measure should be driven by what you value as a business. Other types of performance sometimes measured in addition to task performance include safety-related behaviors, contribution to team performance, and self-development (the use people make of training). Importantly, these aspects of performance should not just be behaviors from a competency model. This is because competency models tend to change every few years, and ideally you want to be able to build up a database of results over many years.

If you are unsure where to start, you can simply measure the following three dimensions (see figure 6.1):

- Task performance (how well objectives are fulfilled)
- Organizational citizenship behavior
- Contribution to team performance

An overall performance score can then be produced by combining the more specific scores, perhaps using a weighting scheme. For example, if you believe that task performance is the most

Figure 6.1 Dimensions of Performance

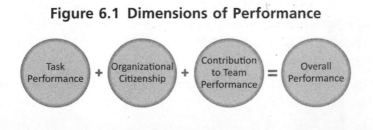

important aspect of overall performance, then you could create an algorithm that reflects this. The rating for task performance could account for, say, 70 percent of overall performance, with contribution to team performance making up 20 percent and citizenship behavior contributing 10 percent.

Of course, as we suggested earlier, these kinds of data are of limited use unless you collect them centrally and connect them with other data. You need to link performance information to results from talent measures. Doing this will enable you to better understand what you are predicting with the talent measures that you use and more precisely ensure that you are measuring all of the factors you need to. But most important, by being more specific about what type of performance you are predicting, you will be able to achieve higher validity levels and thus be better able to accurately identify and measure talent.

Not all organizations will be in a position to implement such a change in how they measure performance. But it need not be complex or time-consuming, and it holds the promise of better measures, better tools, and better people decisions.

Proceeding from a Sound Base

In this chapter, we have looked at the foundational issues that underpin talent measurement. We have distinguished four issues that organizations need to address to ensure that measurement has the impact it should, discussed strategy and policy considerations, and described how businesses can improve the measures and tools available to them through measuring different types of performance. If firms are to go beyond merely using measures that work and instead make measurement work for them, they need to address these issues.

Although not all companies can or need to address all of the issues in this chapter, we are frustrated by just how often we find that even the basic, must-do tasks are not in place. Certainly using a central database, having common data points, and checking whether measures are sufficiently tailored to your company should be no-brainers. They are that easy. Just do it.

The fourth foundation, ensuring proper use, can be a little trickier in some businesses, especially large, diversified, or decentralized ones. Indeed, for some businesses, the issue can seem quite daunting. Yet there are simple things that they can do, and in the next chapter, we look at how organizations can ensure that they use the outputs of measurement—the information provided—to best effect.

7

GETTING THE MOST FROM MEASUREMENT RESULTS

We have to admit it: we are fans of 360-degree feedback, especially when it is used to support performance development. Done well, it can provide access to reinforcing praise, constructive criticism, and developmental suggestions that people otherwise may not receive. It can be a low-cost, high-impact process that adds significant value to both individuals and organizations. And yet few measurement tools are quite as likely to evoke a weary sigh in us as 360s. This is because no other measurement results are probably quite so open to being so utterly unused as 360-degree feedback. We have lost count of the number of times that we have seen people receive a 360 report, read it once, and, then, well . . . nothing. Some may put it in a drawer and file it away for another day. Others may put it in their bag along with good intentions to read it at home or on a train or plane, but somehow they never quite get around to doing so.

Some people, of course, do read, reread, and then act on their 360 report. But without the support of a formal development process, the reality is that most people will not improve their performance as a result of their feedback. It is not that they are not motivated to improve. It is just that the pace and demands of everyday business life get in the way.

Because 360-degree feedback is useful only insofar as businesses and individuals put it to work, it is a perfect example of talent measurement's Achilles' heel. So in this chapter we are going to look at this reality of all talent measurement processes and explore what your business can do to address it. We will see that there are two challenges here. The first is how to ensure that everyone applies the outputs of measurement—the ratings, results, and reports—in an effective way, and not just sometimes but consistently. And the second is how to use the talent intelligence we produce for something more than just guiding individual selection decisions or personal development.

To enable measurement to have its full impact, organizations need to stop overlooking and start acting on both of these challenges. Even among companies that manage to use results consistently well, it is rare to find one that uses the data for something more than just hiring, promoting, or selecting people for high-potential programs. Yet getting these things right represents a huge and important opportunity for businesses to ensure that measurement has the business impact it can and should have.

As an example of what we mean, let us stay with 360s for a moment. In terms of ensuring consistent good use in aiding personal development, some simple things can be done. To begin with, the feedback needs to be useful, by which we mean it should contain specific suggestions on how to develop. So the first step is educating feedback givers on the most helpful type of feedback. This need not involve a long training course but simple, clear, and repeated instructions. In addition, it is essential that there be a formal follow-up process around the 360. For instance, individuals may be required to discuss their report with their manager, agree on key development actions, and then review progress at a later date.

As for using the data for something more, the first step is to collate the data (see chapter 6). Once that is done, firms can start doing things like looking at rating tendencies for each question or competency to check how effectively the 360 is working. If they find that people are always rated very high or low on a particular item, then something may need adjusting. Norm groups or benchmarks can be created, too, which show the average strengths and weaknesses of the company overall or particular business units or teams. And the feedback ratings of high and low performers can be compared to identify which behaviors predict performance and which are most valued by the business. These may not be perfect processes, but they are easy wins that can make all the difference to the value that 360-degree feedback offers.

This, though, is only one tool. How can businesses go about addressing these issues more broadly? In answering this, we will look first at how to use talent measurement results consistently well, before then exploring how to use the data in wider ways and how to build a culture of useful talent measurement within your company.

Using Results Consistently Well

For measurement results to be useful and have an impact, the people applying these results need to do two things with them: understand them and act on them.

Understanding Measurement Results

In some countries, including the United Kingdom, regulations require vendors to sell psychometric tests only to people trained in their use. In South Africa, there is even a law to back this up. Only suitably qualified psychologists are allowed to use these tests. The idea is that psychometrics can be complex and that the people who are using and interpreting the results ought to understand the complexities. It is a laudable idea, yet the reality is that in most countries, measurement results end up in the hands of people who are not trained in the technical complexities of the trade. This is true not only for psychometrics but for all measurement methods and tools. Vendors are aware of this, of course, which is why they produce "manager versions" of test reports to explain and simplify the results for lay users.

The issue remains, though, that the end users of results—business managers, HR managers, and recruiters—often lack a deep understanding of measurement, and this can create problems. Ratings and results may be misinterpreted, and decisions may thereby be misinformed. Many businesses are aware of these risks but are unsure what to do about it. After all, with training programs lasting three to five days and costing thousands of dollars per person, it is not feasible to train everyone who uses results.

Moreover, the widespread availability of preinterpreted results such as manager versions of reports has taken the heat from the issue. The reports appear to provide the support that end users require, especially when combined with access to a trained person should any questions arise. So from most organizations' perspective, no further action seems necessary.

Yet it is, because subtle yet critical misunderstandings about the nature of results persist. Preinterpreted results have helped to a certain extent in terms of assisting end users to understand what specific scores and ratings mean. Yet they are also prone to oversimplifying results and do not help managers understand broader issues about what results are and what they can and cannot tell us. This may sound harmless, but time and again we have seen these issues undermine the way businesses use the results. So doing nothing and relying on preinterpreted reports is not enough. To ensure proper use, businesses need to improve people's understanding of the tools they are using.

The good news is that acting on these issues need not be difficult or time-consuming. We are not talking about large-scale or expensive training initiatives. In fact, many of the associated problems can be avoided by communicating three things to end users: higher scores are not always better; results are estimates, not facts; and beware of oversimplifying results. These could be part of a training program, but they could just as easily be golden rules that are stated every time results are given to end users.

Higher Scores Are Not Always Better. One common misunderstanding is that higher scores are always better. It is, of course, correct that people who score higher on certain measures generally go on to perform better. But the key word here is *generally*. These are general rules. Consider intelligence. We know that it is the single best predictor of success. But a genius may well grow bored in some jobs, and exceptionally high intelligence scores are sometimes accompanied by less desirable qualities—for example, the inability to communicate ideas or think more pragmatically. Similarly, people who score very high on measures of conscientiousness can sometimes come across as inflexible or bureaucratic. And being very high in agreeableness is not always a good thing either, especially in roles that require tough-mindedness. The problem with this misunderstanding that higher is better, then, is that results can be misinterpreted, leaving decisions ill informed.

A related issue here is the risk of homogeneity. One of the problems with companies having a clear view about the type of person they want is that they can end up getting only that type of person. We have seen this in particular when organizations use one of the simpler personality tools that measure only three or four dimensions. Assuming that more is better, these organizations focus on finding people who have these few dimensions in abundance. As a result, they can end up with a bunch of people who are all very similar.

Addressing these issues need not be difficult, but it is important:

- *Communicate the idea.* The rule is simple and easily remembered: more is not always better.
- *Measure fit.* Checking the level of fit between results and role requirements will help shift the focus away from who has the highest scores to who is most likely to meet the demands of particular roles. The check should include the teams individuals will be part of, the managers and stakeholders they will work with, and the wider organizational culture. To ensure it happens, ask HR and

line managers to rate the level of fit between the results and each of these elements. It may not be particularly scientific, but it is quick, easy, and a lot better than doing nothing.

Results Are Estimates, Not Facts. A less simple but equally common misunderstanding is that users will view the results of measures as facts or truths. For example, a job candidate may obtain a low agreeableness score in a personality test, from which a recruiter may conclude that the individual is not agreeable. This sounds reasonable, but it is not because ratings and results are not absolute facts or truths: they are more like estimates.

This is partly because every measure is open to inaccuracies. Assessors may make a wrong judgment, or job applicants may pretend to be something they are not. Part of it, though, is also the fact that how people perform varies from day to day, and when you are assessing them, you do not know if you are catching them on a good day or a bad day. The low agreeableness score, for example, does not mean that someone is not agreeable; rather, it suggests that he or she may tend not to behave this way.

Peter Saville, one of the founding figures of modern measurement, uses the analogy of golf to explain this.[1] As he notes, golfers have a handicap score—a kind of average score that shows how good they are. But on any one day, the score they achieve may not be in line with this handicap. They may do far better than their handicap would suggest one day and far worse the next. Measurement results are pretty much the same. The ratings and results people achieve are determined not only by how good they are, but also by circumstances. As a result, the ideal, most accurate way to show ability is not with a specific score, but with a range of scores. For example, rather than saying that someone has a score of, say, 21 out of 30, it would be better to say that her or his ability can range from 17 to 22.

Of course, without testing someone many times, there is no way for measures to show this range. So it is therefore important

to understand that measurement scores are not perfect indicators; they are just in the ballpark. And it is down to the people
who are reading and interpreting the results to work out where
exactly in the ballpark they are—whether a score is at the top
end of someone's range or the bottom end.

As an example of why this is so important, consider an HR
leader in a large multinational we observed. In addition to the
standard recruitment interviews, the company liked to assess
candidates for senior roles using an individual psychological
assessment process. Yet it had a rule that applicants who achieved
too low a score on an intelligence test were rejected. Never mind
if they had a first-class degree, a track record of success, or specialist technical skills that the business needed. If the person
scored too low, the company ignored all other information and
rejected the person. It was not that this HR leader had researched
what level of intelligence was predictive of high performance. It
was an arbitrary cut-off point. Because the company did not
understand that scores are estimates, it wasted over six thousand
dollars per individual psychological assessment on these candidates by dismissing their application on the basis of just this one
piece of evidence and no doubt missed out on some potentially
good people.

So what should businesses do?

- *Communicate the idea.* Results are estimates, and people
  have ranges, not scores. In our experience, managers know
  what we mean when we use golfing or ballpark analogies to
  explain the issue. Some may not like it, because they would
  prefer to have an easy, quick answer. But they understand
  it, and most prefer to get it right and make good decisions.

- *Cross-reference results.* If someone completes a personality
  test and you have a chance to talk about the result with
  her, do so. Ask if she feels that the results are a true
  reflection and what impact her personality has on her work.
  If someone has an intelligence test, cross-reference his score

with his academic achievement. And if someone attends an individual psychological assessment or assessment center, cross-reference the results with whatever other information you have, such as other interviews.

Beware of Oversimplifying Results. At present, the market tends to present measurement results—and businesses consequently tend to view them—too simplistically. For example, a typical personality test report lists the various dimensions measured and shows an individual's scores. It then briefly explains what these scores mean. A particular sales manager might be high in conscientiousness, low in agreeableness, and about average in everything else. A really good report might point out that conscientiousness is a reasonable predictor of success in sales staff, though slightly less effective for managers.[2] And it may add that having below-average agreeableness is not generally a problem for managers.[3]

What such a report will usually not mention is that the combination of high conscientiousness and low agreeableness is not a good sign. There is some evidence that others may see people with these traits as micromanaging and inflexible.[4] So what is frequently not shown is the interaction among the various factors being measured. Even when interactions are shown for the factors assessed by a single test, they are rarely shown for the factors measured by different tests. We struggle, for instance, to think of an intelligence test report that provides advice on the impact of personality profiles on how people use their intellect.

Similarly, reports from individual psychological assessments, written by consultants for managers, tend not to address interactions either. They typically have one section describing an individual's overall strengths and another describing weaknesses. But they usually do not describe the interplay between these aspects—how one strength affects another, how one weakness exacerbates another, or how a particular strength mitigates a certain weakness.

Why the simplistic view? Well, the ability of experts to interpret the interactions of factors is limited by the fact that researchers have not studied these interplays in great depth. Yet the bigger factor here is that consultants tend to present talent data in the simplest format because that is what the businesses seem to want: as clear and unambiguous a message as possible about the type and level of talent individuals have.

People generally believe that they themselves are complex combinations of qualities and characteristics, yet when it comes to others, they often want a very simple box to put them in, and understandably: managers, who are often the ultimate users of measurement results, are busy enough without having to decipher complex reports. Yet the counterpoint here is that the oversimplification of talent measurement risks ruining it and undermining its potential value to businesses. At a fundamental level, people are complex, and if we ignore this reality, we will inevitably make poor decisions about them.

Yet complexity and clarity are not incompatible. It is perfectly possible to provide more detail and more complex interpretations while also giving a clear message. Managers do not need to become psychologists or test experts; they just need to be aware of the complexities and become educated consumers. Otherwise they risk spending their hard dollars on oversimplified tests that are limited in value and inadvertently misleading.

Importantly, businesses have the power to change this situation:

- *Make sure that measurement results and reports show some of the complexities.* Ask vendors to ensure that preinterpreted results and reports show the interactions between the different qualities and aspects of people. Vendors may not be able to provide all the answers, because the research may not yet have been done. But by asking about these complexities, you will be focusing both you and them on these issues. And in doing so, you will help yourself to make

The Three Cs

The Three Cs is a simple model designed to help people think about and interpret measurement results. As its name suggests, it focuses on three Cs of all measurement results: *contexts*, *consequences*, and *caveats*. So whenever we are told that someone has a particular quality or ability, such as being strongly driven to achieve results, we do not automatically accept this as a good thing. Instead, we ask what the contexts, consequences, and caveats are of this quality are.

So, yes, an individual may be highly driven to achieve tangible results, but in what contexts would this be more or less relevant for performance? For example, it may be essential for a setup role, in which he is establishing a new business stream. But it may be less essential for a maintenance role, which is more about keeping a process running smoothly than achieving targets.

Next come *consequences*: How is the characteristic relevant for performance? In other words, why should we care? How does the characteristic help him perform better? Is it directly, by enabling him to do something better? Or is it indirectly, by affecting other characteristics? For example, the ability to consider and use others' opinions can help people to use their intellect to make decisions.

Finally, there are the *caveats*. What cautions or advisory notices should be given about the person's drive? Under what circumstances would this drive not translate into better performance? What if he is very low on agreeableness? Would he come across as overly pushy and demanding rather than driven? And what if his confidence drops? Will he still be as driven then?

Whenever we are presented with measurement results, then, we look for the Three Cs. It is a simple model that can make a big different in how we interpret and understand people's talents.

better decisions and create market pressure for vendors to develop a better understanding of such interactions.

- *Use a simple model to help managers understand the complexities*. To help end users think about some of the complexities of measurement results, provide a simple model—something catchy and quick to prompt their thinking. The one we frequently use with firms is the Three Cs, which we describe on the previous page.

Acting on Measurement Results

Helping end users understand results is merely the first step in ensuring that measures are consistently used well. Users also need to act on the results effectively. As we mentioned earlier with regard to 360s, it is essential to ensure for developmental assessments that there is some kind of formal follow-up process. Individuals who are not motivated to develop themselves will get only so much out of this, but for those who are motivated to some degree, this kind of support can be essential.

When measurement is used in selection processes, however, ensuring effective action can be trickier. The heart of the matter is the degree to which measurement results influence selection decisions. For example, when measures are used as part of sifting processes, the results usually determine or have a direct impact on the decision about whether to proceed with candidates. In other selection processes, however, the impact of the results is less clear-cut.

We tend to encounter two situations: either businesses and individual leaders overrely on results, always following them no matter what, or they are skeptical about measurement and ignore results if they do not match or confirm how they perceive candidates. This can be about individuals' overconfidence in their own judgment. Often, though, it is about politics and power, about managers wanting to feel they are in control and that it is up to them whom they employ. This is especially so at more senior levels where, ironically, the cost of making a poor decision is higher.

In practical terms, the key issue here is what businesses do when a hiring manager disagrees with measurement results. What happens when a manager thinks yes but the results say no? On the one hand, letting managers ignore the results of measures that the business has invested in seems odd. This is why some businesses have a set policy that these recommendations must be followed. A more covert version of this situation occurs when an influential leader believes in a certain measurement process and managers might feel that they have little option but to follow the results.

On the other hand, there is little point trying to force managers to hire someone they do not want or do not believe in. That rarely ends in success. Moreover, as a matter of principle, we believe that people who are accountable for decisions should be the ones making the decisions. No matter how predictive a measure, the decision maker must always be the one who makes the final decision. A balance is required.

The solution here is to create a sense of accountability for both hiring decisions and how measurement results are used:

- *Communicate clear expectations.* The business should have a clear and simple policy about how measurement results are used. It need not be detailed—for example: "Measurement results provide important information and should be a key part of all recruitment decisions. However, hiring managers are not expected to always follow the results and recommendations of these measures, and are ultimately responsible for the hiring decision."

- *Review hiring decisions.* Whenever a new employee does not work out, both HR and the hiring manager should review the information available at the time of hiring. The goal is not to find fault but to learn lessons that can help prevent the same situation from arising in the future.

- *Track what happens when results and recommendations are both followed and ignored.* When measurement methods deliver a clear hire or no-hire recommendation, both this advice and managers' ultimate hiring decisions should be recorded. These data can be tracked to see what the impact of ignoring measurement results actually is, which can then be relayed to the business.

Man Versus Machine

In 1954 the American psychologist Paul Everett Meehl breathed new life into an old debate when he published a study looking at how medical diagnoses were made.[5] He found that when the results of tests were combined into a diagnosis using statistical methods, the correct diagnosis was achieved more often than when doctors relied only on their clinical judgment. His one caveat was that humans seemed better at identifying unusual bits of information—things that were not part of standard diagnostic tests. But in general, mechanical judgment trumped human judgment.

Although the issue can evoke some passion, the cold, hard facts are that in the half-century since Meehl's work, most of the research has supported his findings. It is not that human judgment cannot be good; in fact, at times it can exceed mechanical judgment. It is simply that human judgment is too unreliable. Sometimes it is great; other times it is not. Mechanical algorithms, though, are always reliable. They are never distracted, never influenced by mood, and never rushed to a premature decision.

One conclusion from this could be that we might be better off doing a series of tests and then plugging the results into an algorithm. Yet it is not quite so simple. In selection decisions, the hiring managers and how they feel about a candidate are a critical part of the equation. And as we have noted, if decision makers are accountable for decisions, they must have the final say.

For measurement to have the impact it should, the outputs and results need to be consistently used effectively. And for this to happen, businesses need to ensure that end users both understand the results and act on them. Organizations can drive this by doing three things. First, they need to communicate a few clear principles about the nature of results and how they should be used. Mass training can be great, but it is not necessary. Good communication and a simple model to help people think about results may be enough. Next, they need to track and review what happens—who makes what decisions and what the outcome is. And, finally, they need to create a sense of accountability for using measurement results.

How measures are applied can be a complex issue, and change certainly cannot be achieved overnight. This is particularly so when organizations have a long tradition of using measures in a certain way. Yet change can come, and the solutions can be quite straightforward. Given this and the cost of not doing anything, we are continually surprised by the number of businesses that seem to have a blind spot here. But businesses must act because investing in measurement solutions without ensuring that they are used properly risks fundamentally undermining their utility and value.

Using Measurement Data to Do More

The vast majority of companies tend to stop here: they focus on ensuring that measurement methods are used effectively to inform and support individual people decisions and development. They tend not to go one step further and use the data for something more. Since much of the potential value of measurement can come from doing this something extra, it is a massive missed opportunity.

By "something more," we mean using measurement data to inform and support processes such as onboarding, talent management, and organizational learning. A recent study found that fewer than 20 percent of companies do this.[6] Even fewer do it effectively or as much as they could.

Although doing this may sound complicated, it tends to be easier than ensuring that managers use measurement results effectively. You do not necessarily need specialist expertise to do it—just a basic comfort with numbers and a good spreadsheet. That, and the will to do it.

Linking Measurement to Onboarding

Probably the easiest win here is for businesses to link the outputs of recruitment assessments to onboarding. It may sound obvious, but it is done surprisingly infrequently. Indeed, one of the most common mistakes that companies make with new employees is to assume that they will need little support to integrate well and get up to speed.[7] To us, it seems odd to go to great lengths to identify candidates' strengths and weaknesses and then not to use this information to ensure that they are successful. Yet in many businesses, the idea that a candidate may require support tends to be viewed as a weakness and raises questions about suitability. So the challenge here is partly about readjusting expectations so that providing support is a common part of onboarding.

Even when hiring managers want to provide support, creating a development plan for new employees can be difficult, not least because managers lack information about them. This is where measurement can come in. Even if the only method businesses use is interviews, measurement processes can provide key bits of information to help direct onboarding support. This can be simple, consisting of nothing more than giving interview notes to managers (especially when interviewers are asked to suggest what onboarding support candidates may require). Or it can be more sophisticated, with the outputs of interviews and other measurement methods being fed to both the hiring manager and an onboarding team. Either way, it is a big and easy win.

- *Collect the information.* Make sure the selection process captures candidates' strengths and weaknesses so that you can use this information to support new people. It should not be onerous. As interviewers almost always form ideas about what level of support candidates might require, it is merely a matter of recording them.

- *Have an onboarding process.* This can be as uncomplicated as a meeting between the new employee and the manager to agree on an onboarding plan.

- *Review progress.* Hold a follow-up session to review the new employee's integration after sixty or ninety days.

Talent Analytics

Probably the biggest win to be achieved from applying measurement data lies in talent analytics. Again, this may sound complicated, but it is just about using the data to inform other people processes, such as talent management or learning and leadership development.

A global business asked us to help it establish measurement processes to support three key people decisions: the recruitment of new employees, identification of people with high potential, and selection for promotion. The processes created were not complex. They mostly involved interviews, supported at more junior levels by sifting methods and at senior levels by individual psychological assessment. But they were implemented with all data centrally collected and just one competency framework used across the business. As a result, we were able to use these simple data to do far more than merely support people decisions:

○ *We looked at the competency ratings of new employees in each business division.* This enabled us to ask two questions: Were some divisions attracting stronger candidates than others? And were the qualities of new employees aligned with each unit's business objectives? Sure enough, two divisions appeared to be attracting lower-quality candidates. Another unit, whose strategy involved fast organic growth, was hiring relatively risk-averse people. As a result of these findings, all three divisions were able to change their attraction and hiring activities.

○   *We compared the average competency ratings of new employees with those of the people nominated as those with high potential.* We found that the new people had an uncannily similar pattern of strengths and weaknesses to the current employees. This led to a debate in the business about whether it was "just employing clones," which eventually led to changes in the hiring process.

○   *Allied to this, we compared the average ratings of new employees with those of applicants who were not selected.* We found that what most distinguished those who were not selected was that they tended to be extroverts and less risk averse. This reinforced the finding that the company was employing clones.

○   *We were able to look at the qualities that distinguished those identified as having high potential and those being promoted.* We found that the people labeled as high potential were generally better at performing well, being outgoing, and showing entrepreneurial spirit. In a business trying to adopt a faster-paced, edgier, and more entrepreneurial approach, this was a good finding. But when we looked at the qualities most likely to lead to promotion, we found something slightly different. When it came to actual career progression, it seemed that the people being chosen were those who performed well and were viewed as team players. For all the encouragement the business was trying to give people with the qualities it thought it wanted, the people being promoted into leadership roles were different. As a result of these findings, the business developed new criteria for promotion.

○   *Finally, we looked at the average competency profiles of the groups measured and fed the findings into the learning and leadership development functions.* As a result, specific learning and development programs were created to address key competency weaknesses in particular groups of employees. The measurement data thus enabled better targeting of learning and development investment.

These were all simple steps, accomplished with simple data and without resorting to expensive systems. But they led to powerful findings that ultimately helped the business deliver its growth strategy.

A less simple and more headline-grabbing example of using data to achieve more is closed-loop analytics: connecting measurement results with key talent and business performance data points—things like sales revenue, customer service scores, performance ratings, absenteeism, and even bonuses. This may sound daunting, but it is really a matter of collecting the data in one place. Specialist systems do exist and can help considerably, but a large spreadsheet will also do the job.

The data can then be used to identify the impact of each measure on different business outcomes. For example, it might be found that targeting particular personality profiles is associated with lower levels of employee theft. As a result, businesses are able to do two things. They can adjust and improve the measures they use to be able to predict certain outcomes more accurately. And since they will have a better understanding of what measures predict which outcomes, they will be able to adjust their hiring practices to target particular types of candidates.

We have seen a couple of companies go one step further and connect four data points: measurement results, talent data, business metrics, and employee engagement data. They can then see, for example, exactly how various leadership behaviors affect engagement and performance.

However, as we have argued, although smart systems can be great, they are not always necessary. As a recent McKinsey report noted, simply making data more accessible to relevant stakeholders can create tremendous value.[8] In this vein, at the company described earlier, we developed annual measurement data reports at the group, divisional, and functional levels. The frequency of reporting should obviously depend on the amount of measurement activity in a business. In our experience, though, the key is to have a reporting period that allows new insights with each report. Producing quarterly reports is possible, but if each new one does not provide new insights, this risks undermining the perceived value of the reports.

As we have seen, measurement data can be used for so much more than individual people decisions and development. Precisely what will depend on your business, but we hope that the examples will provide you with ideas and inspiration. We had originally hoped to give many more examples, with case studies showcasing the companies that excel at this. But the more we investigated, the more we realized that the majority of organizations are not currently leveraging their measurement data to provide this "something extra." This is a shame, because in every case, it is a missed opportunity. If the rise of Web search engines has taught us nothing else, it has taught us that we should collect, connect, and use data.

Things are changing slowly. In this emerging era of big data, companies are trying to leverage all the information they can get to better understand and improve the way their businesses function. Talent analytics is one of the latest frontlines of this data-driven push for profits, with the promise of talent intelligence held out as the prize. Yet as we noted at the beginning of this book, these systems tend not to include measurement data. This is a critical point because measurement results are the key to turning plain old administrative talent data into genuine talent intelligence.

Measurement brings the ability not only to know the talents and competency profiles of people but also to achieve more effective and targeted hiring, promotion, and development pro-cesses. It also affords the opportunity to use these processes to change and develop the competencies of different employee groups to match, support, and drive business objectives.

Building a Culture of Measurement

Of course, building talent intelligence takes time. Initial insights are possible, but it usually takes a year or so to be able to start seeing trends. And although taking steps to ensure that people use results well can have an immediate impact, it often takes some years to achieve fully.

Perhaps this is why so many businesses do not focus on these issues: they seem too long term. But we cannot say too many times that businesses should focus on them. Measurement is useless unless the results are used well, and businesses are extract-ing only half of the value that measurement has to offer if they do not do more with the data.

Moreover, by pursuing these things, a tipping point can be reached, at which understanding and expectations about mea-surement change. People come to understand what they can and cannot do with results and assume and expect more from the data. And it is this self-sustaining culture of measurement, not just operational logistics, that should be a key goal of implementing measurement processes. Getting the measure to the participant and the results to the manager is the easy bit. Building the culture is the challenge. And every use of measurement is an opportunity to change the way people think about it and treat it.

A few years ago, we met a global financial services business that claimed to have built a culture of measurement. Impressed, we explored further. We found that there was indeed an expecta-tion that measurement should be an integral part of people decisions, as well as a widespread belief that it could add value. But there was no real attempt to ensure consistent use and only a limited effort to use the data to do more. So whatever culture of measurement existed was limited. Yet it did raise an interesting point: for some businesses, achieving such a culture seems a long way off and simply getting managers to accept the use of measurement can be a big win. For companies in this situation, we have found that three simple steps invariably work to begin moving the business toward measurement: show the business case; start small, get it right, and then expand; and get the interviews right.

Show the Business Case

Sometimes the challenge is as fundamental as convincing managers that they need help and that measurement can provide it. Other times it is simply about showing that measurement need not slow selection processes down or lead to lost candidates. Whatever the specific issue, the answer is always the same: build a compelling business case that senior executives can buy into. The place to begin is with hard data on the current situation— things like failure rates and average performance ratings of new employees. Of course, sometimes these figures do not show any need for measurement. It could be that turnover is generally low and performance ratings are uniformly high. Or it may be that people decisions are already pretty good and the business simply wants to improve them further. In these cases, there is plenty of evidence freely available about the positive impact that measurement can have when done well. Either way, the first step in introducing measurement is to establish evidence of why the business needs it.

Start Small, Get It Right, and Then Expand

We are often asked which measurement processes should be introduced first. Our answer is to start with the process that is most likely to yield the biggest benefit, but begin with a small trial. Use this trial to hone it, tweak it, and get it working well, and only then expand it elsewhere in the business. The trial period will also provide an opportunity to evaluate the process and build evidence of its value, and the senior leaders involved can become champions for the process.

Get Interviews Right

Probably the most frequent touch point that managers have with measurement is the hiring interview. So even if a firm's objective is to introduce psychometrics to selection processes, it needs to make sure that it gets interviews right. This is partly because any positive impact of testing will be limited if the accompanying interviews are not done well. But it is also because getting interviews right provides an ideal opportunity to educate the business at large about some of the basics of measurement—things like the value of being better at measurement, the risks of rating biases, and the benefits of focusing on fit.

So how can business get interviews right? The subject is worthy of a book, but there are five main levers to use:

1. *Communication with the candidate*. Good communication equals a better candidate experience. As with all other measurement processes, then, it is important that candidates know exactly what to expect when they come for an interview.

2. *Training for interviewers*. All interviewers should be given basic information about regulatory compliance—whether there are any questions they have to ask and what kinds of things they are not legally allowed to ask. Beyond this, though, training can help ensure that interviewers make better judgments and provide a better candidate experience.

Some companies choose to teach interviewers about building rapport and asking different sets of questions. Another current vogue is to educate interviewers on potential biases that they may have and that can reduce the quality of their judgments. Both types of training can help. But there is evidence to suggest that if companies do only one piece of interviewer training, it should be frame-of-reference training: providing interviewers with examples of interviews and then getting them to rate the interviewee.[9] The idea is that this helps create a common reference point for what good looks like.

As for who to train, obviously the more people you train the better, but there is another option. One thing we have seen some businesses do when candidates have more than one interview is to focus on training a small cadre of "superinterviewers": individuals who are trained in interviewing skills to a higher level than other people in the company. They then ensure that every candidate is seen by one of these superinterviewers.

3. *Interview guides*. Preset lists of questions for interviewers to ask are useful because they provide a process to follow. They can thus ensure consistency, as well as give interviewers suggestions for questions. Most textbooks will tell you that structured interviews are what you need. But as we explained in chapter 4, they are not always the best option. By far the preferred option, especially at middle or senior levels, is the semistructured interview. It provides interviewing managers with an opportunity to build rapport and gives candidates a much better experience.

4. *Interview outputs*. The typical outputs of interviews are comments and ratings. We know of some businesses in which there simply are no outputs from interviews: no notes are taken, no formal comments given, and no ratings made. We also know of other businesses that require detailed notes to be taken and a page or two of comments and ratings to be made afterward. In our experience, a compromise between these extremes works best. Some ratings need to be made and some brief comments can be helpful to the hiring manager or HR. But these should be kept to a minimum. Managers are busy

people, and only information that is going to be subsequently used should be recorded.

5. *Accountability*. Finally, businesses need to ensure that interviewers feel accountable for their judgments. The flip side of this is that good interviewers should be praised and rewarded. Interviewing is a valuable skill for businesses, and it should be treated as such.

One final point about interviews is that businesses also have the option to buy a ready-made solution like an interview system. This combines interview guides and training in how to do interviews. Some of the interview guides have set structures; others are flexible and can be tailored. They are attractive because they can appear to be a quick route to improving interviews, and some of them are genuinely good. But they are also short-term solutions and, in our experience, are usually overpriced for what they are, in particular those that require all users to be "certified." Instead, it tends to be cheaper and better to use independent consultants to build your own interview guides and provide training. There is certainly no need to tie yourself into using inflexible systems that require interviewers to be certified. So if you are serious about interviews, build your own. It can be as effective as any off-the-shelf interview system and will be more tailored and considerably cheaper.

Spreading the Expertise

Using measurement results and data effectively, then, is about building a culture of measurement. It is about changing perceptions in the business at large about what measurement is and can do. In this respect, measurement expertise should be distributed throughout the business rather than residing in a few individuals. We do not mean here that everyone needs to be a trained expert, just that the business end users of measurement methods should be effective, educated consumers.

Of course, some specialist expertise will still be required, be that an internally employed expert or external consultants or vendors. And this is the topic that we address in the next chapter: how organizations can source the expertise they need to implement and use measurement methods.

Standardizing Interviews Across a Decentralized Global Business

Improving measurement processes need not always be expensive or involve complex technologies. A few years ago, we worked with a large global business in the energy sector, helping it develop its measurement practices. One of the issues we quickly uncovered was that both how interviews were done and how well they were done varied considerably across the business.

To ensure interviews were consistently effective, we wanted to introduce a common process, a standardized way of doing them. Yet the company was hugely decentralized, with a culture of every business unit doing its own thing. And it quickly became clear that there was no budget for training interviewers.

In talking to frontline HR staff and managers, we discovered that almost everyone seemed to struggle with the questions to ask in interviews. To address this, we developed a new interview process. At the heart of it was a single interview guide that could be used for all nontechnical interviews at all levels of the business.

Created in a simple Microsoft Excel spreadsheet, it presented users with a simple form. All they had to do was provide four pieces of information:

- Which country the role was within
- What level of the business the role was in
- Whether it was a people management or individual contributor role
- Which four of sixteen competencies were most critical for success in the role

CASE STUDY

Users then pressed the Print button, and an interview guide appeared. It had a standardized structure, with instructions for how to conduct the interview. It provided suggestions for introductory questions to build rapport with the applicant. It listed the questions that legally had to be asked. Then for each of the four selected competencies, the interview guide suggested five questions, with users being advised to select just two or three. Each question was accompanied by follow-on prompts and behavioral indicators— suggestions of what a good and a poor answer might look like to guide the rating of competencies. Finally, there was space for notes and a form requiring certain ratings and comments to be made.

In total, there were 480 main questions, with many more follow-ons, and a similar number of behavioral indicators. This may sound complicated and expensive, but it was not. To build it, we first asked a vendor to provide a list of questions and behavioral indicators. Since the vendor already had such a list for its own generic competency frameworks, it was not difficult to prepare this. All it had to do was match the competencies in the company's framework with its own. We then asked a second vendor to check and add to the list. Finally, we reviewed the list ourselves before asking a specialist in Excel to build a spreadsheet to contain all the information. All in all, it cost under twelve thousand dollars.

It succeeded because it made life easier for people, so the business wanted to use it. It was simple and easy to use. The Excel format meant that it could be used anywhere in the world. And the standardized structure meant that a more or less common interview process was followed across the business.

It did not solve all issues, of course. Training was still lacking. It was a good start, though, and it bought us the goodwill and credibility with frontline managers that we needed to do more to improve interviews. We did a lot of things at that company to develop its measurement processes, some of them quite expensive and technical. But in retrospect, it was this simple tool that probably had the biggest impact of all, touching as it did almost every manager in the firm.

8

SOURCING THE EXPERTISE
YOU NEED

Deep down, buried beneath all the challenges and opportunities of measurement that we have described, lurks a pointed question: How do you source the expertise you need to do it all?

Measurement is—or at least should be—a technical business. So to do it well, sooner or later you either need to have technical expertise yourself or access to someone else who does.

We call it a "pointed" issue because organizations often struggle with it. Many, especially smaller firms, lack internal expertise and so rely on external experts. Yet choosing and managing technical vendors when you do not have expertise yourself has its challenges. An increasing number of larger companies therefore employ internal experts. This approach is not devoid of challenges either. For starters, there is more than one type of measurement expertise, and knowing which you need is not always clear. Then there is the matter of how best to position, structure, and deploy this resource.

In this chapter, we look at these issues. They are critical because without access to the right expertise in the right places, decisions made about whether and how to do measurement are unlikely to be sufficiently informed. And in our experience, the single biggest factor holding businesses back from making measurement work better for them is a lack of understanding.

We begin by looking at the options in sourcing expertise. We then turn to the issue of how to select, contract with, and manage vendors.

Sources of Expertise

Organizations have four basic options when it comes to sourcing the expertise they need to select, manage, and use measurement:

- Use vendors.
- Appoint independent, freelance consultants.
- Train HR personnel.
- Employ their own experts.

Many small to medium-sized businesses have little choice in how they approach the issue. The extent of their measurement use does not justify employing an expert in the field or training internal personnel, so they have to rely on external vendors.

For slightly larger businesses, however, there are two additional options. First, they can train key personnel (usually HR) in particular methods or tools. For example, HR managers are often trained in the use of psychometric tests. This enables the informed use of particular tests and saves money in the long term by avoiding the need to use external vendors.

But no matter how skilled these individuals may be in the use of certain methods or tests, this kind of training does not provide deeper technical expertise or a broad overview of the market. So another option for companies, which is increasingly common, is to have an independent expert help them navigate the measurement market. These are specialists who have worked in the field for a while and are familiar with the vendors in it. Their role is different from that of vendors in that they act only as advisors and do not become involved in delivery. They typically assist firms in identifying who and what to measure and which vendors and tools to use. They can also advise on how best to extract value from the outputs. Obviously their involvement adds to overall costs. The benefit of using them is that it can help ensure that the investment in measurement is money well spent.

For larger businesses, there is another option: employing their own experts.

There are five types of role that technical experts often play within organizations:

○ *Deliverer*. A few large organizations have their own in-house assessment delivery teams. Sometimes they focus only on a particular process, such as running assessment centers for graduates. At other times, they may deliver a range of services. Research into the cost benefits of in-house delivery is limited, but it appears to be no more expensive than using good external vendors. The main benefit of employing in-house teams is the extra control it brings over quality. There is also a suggestion that since these people have better knowledge of the business, they can make better judgments about how well individuals fit, although no definitive research has yet been done to test this assumption. Moreover, since this in-house role offers less variety than a similar role with a vendor, firms may struggle to attract and retain the best assessors.

○ *Designer*. Although it is increasingly rare, some organizations design their own methods and tools. The most common elements designed are interviews, assessment centers, and 360-degree feedback tools. Rarely, companies may also design their own psychometrics. The role, often combined with a delivery role, obviously requires considerable technical expertise.

○ *Manager*. More common is appointing in-house experts to project-manage measurement processes and oversee the work of vendors. These individuals are usually in middle-level positions in the center of businesses, although they are sometimes employed by specific business units. The role rarely touches on measurement strategy; instead, it focuses on specific measurement projects or processes. The idea of using experts rather than generic project managers is that their expertise will enable them to ensure better outcomes are achieved. One common risk here, though, can occur when a vendor is appointed and championed by a senior executive. The vendor may believe that it reports to this individual rather than to the expert, thus compromising the expert's role. In our experience, therefore, this role can deliver real value only when manager-experts have genuine control and authority over the activities of vendors.

○   *Broker.* The internal broker role sometimes contains elements of the manager role, but it also involves the expert acting as an internal consultant. The role is typically positioned at the center of a business and is often referred to as a center of expertise. Brokers are a resource for the whole business and can advise on all matters relating to measurement. A common scenario is for a business unit or team to ask for assistance in obtaining a particular measurement process or tool. A broker can then consult on what type of solution will meet the business's need and help select and purchase the best tool or service. The role can therefore provide a useful lever for driving consistent practice across a business. Brokers can set standards, ensure good data collection, and promote effective use of measurement results at a local level.

○   *Strategic owner.* The final, increasingly common role filled by experts is that of the strategic owner of talent measurement. It often includes elements of the manager and broker roles but extends beyond them. Strategic owners are responsible for developing an organization's measurement strategy and policies. They often own many or all of the organization's assessment processes. And, critically, they are responsible for leveraging measurement data to inform other people processes. The big benefit the role brings is that longer-term and cross-unit interests, such as the creation of talent intelligence, can be better served.

For the strategic owner role to deliver these benefits, however, two things need to be true. First, the person must be both a measurement expert, with deep technical understanding, and a skilled organizational operator who can influence at senior levels. It is increasingly common for nonspecialists to head up HR areas, including talent management and learning. Whether this is ever advisable for any area is debatable, but for measurement it absolutely is not. No other area is quite so pervaded by deeply technical issues. And unless individuals understand them, their effectiveness will be compromised.

Second, the role must be positioned correctly in the organizational structure. It is important that strategic owners sit outside any recruitment, learning or development teams. This is because when they reside within one of these teams, the role invariably becomes siloed within that team. For example, we know one head of assessment who works in a large global corporation and reports to the recruitment director. The intention was for his role to focus on all aspects of measurement, not just hiring. But since the learning and development heads view him as part of recruitment and want to retain control of their own areas, they tend to avoid working through him whenever possible.

Even when experts are employed at a supposedly senior— and therefore more strategic—level, their role often ends up being fairly tactical in nature. And it is this lack of expertise at a genuinely senior level that accounts for many of the implementation issues we have described. It is why strategy is often missing, why data are so infrequently used, and why practice tends to vary across firms. Far too few large businesses that have expertise have it in the right places.

Types of Experts

Part of the reason that companies lack sufficient technical expertise has been their lack of understanding of the value that talent
measurement can add over and above merely supporting individual people decisions. Seen as a tactical and almost operational
issue, it has been treated and positioned as such. Another part
of the reason, though, is the dearth of suitable expertise. On the
face of things, there is no shortage of experts, but finding one
with the right mix of skills is not always easy.

Groups of Experts

One way to think about the type of expertise required is to consider three overlapping groups of experts: industrial/occupational
psychologists, psychometricians, and consultants:

○ *Industrial/occupational psychologists (I/OPs)*. Psychologists who specialize in operating in businesses are known
as industrial or occupational psychologists and they are
often certified by national associations. Their training, and
therefore their overall approach, is primarily driven by
research and theory. There are two main communities of
I/OPs: academics, who work in universities and business
schools and undertake most of the research, and
practitioners, who work in consultancies or directly for
companies. As a profession, they bring deep technical
knowledge and a broad understanding of the various
measurement methods. Yet they are often accused of
lacking pragmatism and of overly focusing on best practice
at the expense of fit-for-purpose practice. An example of
this is their advocacy of structured interviews described in
chapter 4. In our experience, this characterization is
probably not fair for the profession as a whole. Indeed,
some of the profession's own most prominent members

have spoken out on the issue, agreeing with much of the criticism. Yet as with all other professions, there is much variability in I/OPs, and some of them can be very pragmatic and commercial.

○ *Psychometricians*. As the name suggests, psychometricians typically specialize in the development of psychometric tests. They are often I/OPs but can also be mathematicians. As a group, they probably have a deeper understanding of the technicalities of measurement than anyone else. Yet few have business experience, and fewer still have the ability to explain complex technicalities in simple terms that business users can understand. As a result, the consultancies employing them often keep them away from clients, and they are rarely employed by businesses directly. However, if you can find a good psychometrician with an appreciation of the realities of operating within a corporate environment and the ability to explain the mathematical complexities of measurement in easily understandable terms, then you have found the holy grail of measurement expertise.

○ *Consultants*. Like psychometricians, consultants are often I/OPs. Other types of psychologists, such as educational, forensic, and counseling psychologists, are common. Some vendors also employ nonpsychologists who are trained in measurement methods. We know of one large global vendor, for example, that advocates the qualities of former priests. Another employs mainly ex-businesspeople. These varied backgrounds mean that consultants can lack some of the technical knowledge that I/OPs bring, yet they can make up for this with their experience of implementing measurement processes.

Understanding the differences among these groups can be useful, but when trying to select individuals to employ, it can be more useful to think in terms of competencies. We typically identify five:

- Technical knowledge
- Consulting experience in delivering and implementing a variety of measurement processes in a range of businesses
- Pragmatism and commerciality (commercial experience— the ability to operate effectively within organizations)
- Credibility at senior levels of a business
- Market knowledge

Using these qualities, we can identify the type of individual needed to fulfill each of the five key measurement roles described above (see table 8.1).

Finding the Right Mix

As with any other role, it is important to find people with the right mix of experience and abilities. The most common challenge here is obtaining people who have both technical expertise

Table 8.1 Competency Requirements of the Five Core Measurement Roles

Role	Competencies				
	Technical Understanding	Consulting Experience	Business Experience	Senior Credibility	Market Knowledge
Deliverer	O	X	O	O	—
Designer	X	O	O	—	X
Manager	X	X	X	O	O
Broker	O	X	O	O	X
Strategic owner	X	X	X	X	X

X = highly desirable. O = nice to have. — = not required.

and business experience. The crux of this issue is often seen to be the apparent gap that exists between the scientific I/OP world and the commercial, pragmatic business world. Fairly or unfairly, firms tend to view I/OPs as being more focused on making measures that are as good as possible at measuring than on making ones that help businesses work better. The I/OP training institutions show little inclination to change their approach, however. And why should they? They would argue that their job is to produce professionals who know about I/OP, not to produce people for businesses. Since the issue is unlikely to be resolved anytime soon, businesses need to find their own solutions.

One obvious option is to employ junior-level I/OPs and then promote them, gradually teaching them how to operate in a business just like anyone else. But since few firms have large I/OP teams that give room for progression, this is not usually a viable option. An alternative is to employ "second-jobbers": I/OPs who have obtained some initial business experience in other organizations. Yet this option, while more viable for many businesses, is limited by the relatively small size of the I/OP job market.

Finally, there is the option of employing consultants in-house. The idea is that they may not have experience of operating in business, but they do have experience of operating in partnership with companies and tend to be fairly pragmatic. However, they can be difficult to attract, and the transition for consultants is not always easy, since the qualities needed to succeed in corporate environments tend to be different from those required in consultancies.

Because finding the right people is not always easy, many firms effectively outsource measurement. It is not an ideal solution because there are some things that external vendors cannot do. Evaluating their own work, for one, cannot—or at least should not—be left to them. They also cannot manage results and link them with a company's other talent data. Moreover, although many aspects of measurement can be outsourced, there are still the issues of how to choose and work most effectively with vendors. And when a firm has no other access to measurement expertise, doing this well can be difficult. Yet there are things you can do.

Using Vendors

The vast majority of businesses that we have worked with rely at least to some degree on external providers. In fact, studies show that measurement is among the most frequently outsourced of all HR activities. There is nothing wrong with this: it can be an effective strategy. The big *but* here is that outsourcing is effective only when businesses know how to select, contract, and manage measurement vendors.

In the rest of this chapter, we present some simple guidelines on how to do each of these three things. Before we do so, though, let us briefly look at the state of the market today.

The State of the Market

The sheer number of vendors is staggering. The choice seems endless. Historically, however, they have divided into two clear groups. On the one side, there have been specialist psychometric and 360-degree feedback vendors, which primarily create and sell tests and tools. On the other side have been the general measurement consultancies, which do things like run assessment centers and provide individual psychological assessments, but get involved in almost everything related to measuring and developing talent (see table 8.2).

The line between these two camps has always been blurred (Cubiks, for example, specializes in psychometrics and 360-degree feedback systems). But the downturn that began in 2007 has seen the line become ever less distinct.

Many measurement firms have fared well during the downturn, fueled by business restructurings and increased caution in hiring decisions. Not everyone has done well, of course. The

Table 8.2 Examples of the Two Groups of Vendors

Specialist Vendors	Generalist Vendors
SHL (previously known as Saville & Holdsworth, now US owned)	DDI (US-based, global, privately owned firm)
OPP (which operates in the United States in partnership with CPP and ipat)	PDI (US based and global)
Saville Consulting (formed by one of the founders of SHL)	YSC (UK based and global)
TalentQ (formed by the other founder of SHL)	Cubiks (Europe based and global)

general consultancies seemed to have fared better than the specialist psychometric and 360-degree feedback vendors. And because of the sensitive nature of restructuring, businesses have tended to use trusted big-name vendors, leaving many of the smaller firms struggling. There has thus been some consolidation within the industry, with a gradual trend for larger firms to buy smaller providers.

However, the market space was radically changed by new entrants in 2011 and 2012. In 2011, two of the biggest specialist psychometric vendors, SHL and Previsor, merged in a long-predicted deal. Then, in mid-2012, a company previously unknown in the measurement space, the Corporate Executive Board, bought both the now giant SHL-Previsor and a respected US general measurement firm called Valtera.

At the same time, search firms have been developing their measurement businesses in an effort to diversify their income. Korn/Ferry, in particular, has gone on a buying spree, acquiring personnel and a number of smaller businesses, before acquiring the once market leader in assessment, PDI. Other search firms such as Heidrick & Struggles and Egon Zender have followed suit, though they appear more focused on the organic growth of their existing measurement businesses. The expansion of these firms has not just been about size: their products and services have expanded as well. Traditionally they operated at an entirely different price point to the specialist assessment and development consultancies, charging two to three times as much. Some still do this, too, although there is no evidence that we are aware of that these higher costs equate to better predictive validities. Many of them, however, launched new services and products priced to compete directly with the mainstream measurement market. Whether they will be successful remains to be seen. For example, we know of many HR people who strongly believe that headhunting firms should not be let anywhere near their talent and that measurement and search should be kept independent. Search firms would argue that their assessment businesses are separate from their headhunting arms. Yet we suspect that the reservations of many HR professionals will remain and thereby limit headhunters' role in the market. Nonetheless, they are players and have a growing chunk of the market.

Finally, hovering on the edge of this picture are two groups. First, there are the persistent rumors that some of the big business consultancies might try to move into the measurement market through a large acquisition. Second, there are the twin peaks of IBM and Oracle. In 2012 each completed a high-profile purchase of a company combining a talent acquisition system (for managing recruitment processes) with measurement products (IBM purchased Kenexa, and Oracle bought Taleo). Many specialist psychometric providers are keeping a careful eye on these developments, and some appear to be diversifying into the general measurement consultancy space as a contingency.

So there has been a lot of movement in the market, and there is likely to be more. The general thrust seems to be that many medium-sized firms have been bought or squeezed out, leaving a mix of larger consultancies and quite small ones. These smaller firms are generally too small for their bigger counterparts to worry about, but their lower cost base means that they can be attractive to organizations.

The current round of consolidation is undoubtedly overdue and promises to cohere what has historically been a fragmented market. It is something we welcome and see as good news for organizations, making it easier for them to navigate the market and choose which product and vendor to use. Yet as independent observers of the field, we also view the current round of consolidations with some concern, as there is a noticeable trend among many of the new entrants to the market to monetize the intellectual capital of measurement firms through promoting generic and global products.

This approach can certainly make choosing assessment products easier for companies. But the problem with this approach, as we showed in chapter 3, is that the more generic measures are, the less likely they are to achieve high validities and help businesses measure fit. Our concern therefore is that the intervention of new players without a long tradition in what is a very specialist technical arena will bring with it a raft of generic, off-the-shelf monetized products and services that look good but are not that effective.

How to Select Vendors

How, then, should businesses choose a vendor? The subject is worthy of a book in its own right, and the criteria used vary by businesses and products. Yet a couple of general principles are worth noting.

Conduct a Proper Selection Process. One of the most common mistakes companies make when selecting vendors is not following a proper process. Lacking technical understanding and faced with an overwhelming number of options, many HR and business leaders have a favorite vendor or tool that they seek to use whenever possible. The selection process can thus become a cover for selecting a preordained favorite. This is bad business in any procurement process, and no less so for measurement.

Without genuine competition among vendors, the likelihood of achieving high-quality, cost-effective solutions is distinctly reduced. So follow a proper process. The precontest favorite may well still win, but the competition will put the true value of its bid in perspective.

Select a Measure, Not a Vendor. A related issue is that because they lack expertise in the field, some businesses simply choose the vendor with which they feel they have the best chemistry. From a business's point of view, it is not entirely a bad idea. One of our core rules is to ask ourselves whether, if things go horribly wrong, we would trust a vendor to stand beside us and deal with the problem. This kind of trust or chemistry factor is a valid selection criterion, but it must not be the only or main one. Organizations must also investigate the quality of the products or services they are purchasing. This is partly about making sure that what they buy measures precisely what it is intended to. Chapters 2 to 4 should help in determining this. It is also partly about questioning the validity of measures. This is especially important given the increasing evidence of reporting bias: the tendency for some vendors, while presenting validities as scientific, to report these figures selectively in a way that overstates the effectiveness of their tools. The guide to questioning validity we presented in chapter 5 can help here. No matter how you do it, though, it is important not to assume that measures are effective or to take vendors' claims at face value. Always question them.

Look for Expertise. Although we have just said you should focus more on the measure than on the vendor, one critical aspect of vendors is their level of expertise. With individual psychological assessment in particular, it is arguably more important to choose the right assessors than to focus on the measurement process. (For more on how to select an individual psychological assessment vendor, see the appendix.) With smaller vendors, look for people who have come from bigger, more established providers. For example, the founders of the UK-based VesseyHopperMcVeigh all learned their trade at SHL. In larger vendors, individuals' backgrounds are also important, but another useful source of insight can be the origins of the business overall, since mergers and acquisitions can hide who you are really buying from. For instance, IBM's acquisition Kenexa is more known for its talent acquisition systems, but in 2006 Kenexa purchased a reputable psychometrics firm called PSL. And although some people may not have heard of Cubiks (one of the larger global vendors), its origins lie in PA Consulting Group, one of the world's best-known management consultancies.

Reputations and backgrounds are not always what they appear to be, of course. One or two large psychometrics vendors seem to have dined out on their reputation for quite a time now, even though their tests have since been overtaken by newer, better tools. Yet for businesses that do not have technical expertise and need to acquire it, reputations can be a useful indicator.

Do Not Select Only on the Basis of Price. At the risk of repeating ourselves, measurement is a precision instrument. Purchasing only on price is like buying a supercar on the cheap and still expecting it to be super. There is a degree to which the cost simply is what the cost is. For example, we have seen many organizations seek to drive down the cost of individual psychological assessments, only for vendors to respond by putting less experienced, cheaper consultants in place. You get what you pay for. This does not mean that price is not important. Businesses obviously need to secure the most cost-effective solution possible. But those that select only on the basis of price invariably are stung on quality.

How to Contract with Vendors

Some companies place a strong focus on selecting vendors and then seem to view contracting as a formality. But often it is not.

And if they get it wrong, the relationship with the vendor will rarely go right. Larger companies have a legal or procurement department to help with this. Indeed, for these businesses, we recommend simplifying matters by using a standard contract with all measurement vendors. Smaller firms, though, usually have to rely on the contracts presented by vendors. Whichever route is used, there are a number of key issues to bear in mind to avoid the most common pitfalls in contracting with suppliers.

To some, what we write below may sound a little harsh. Yet this is not our intention and, indeed, we firmly believe that contracts must be fair to all parties. We are just trying to be clear, and if contracts do nothing else, they should make things clear.

Intellectual Property Rights. A number of years ago, one of the best-known global measurement vendors signed a contract with one of the world's largest oil and gas suppliers to produce a new leadership framework for them. Unfortunately the energy firm either did not check the details of the contract or did not understand what they meant: the contract assigned the intellectual property rights (IPR) in the framework to the vendor and prevented the business from using the framework with any other vendors. As a result, the firm was effectively tied to using that vendor for all measurement activity at leadership levels. The only way it can stop using the vendor is to create a new leadership framework.

Intellectual property rights are vital, and some of the biggest vendors are some of the worst culprits here. There are two simple guiding rules. First, if a business pays for the design of a new measure that is not based on something in which the vendor already owns the IPR, then the IPR for the new measure should belong to the business. No debate, no exceptions. If a business pays for the development of a new 360-degree feedback tool or situational judgment tests, then the questions that the tool comprises should belong to the business. The IT system that the tool is delivered on still belongs to the vendor, but the questions should belong to the business. By all means, share the IPR for the questions with the vendor, but do not merely give them to it. There should be no ties that bind. If a vendor does not do its job well, firms should be free to walk away. Moreover, if a vendor develops a tool for you at your expense, do you really want it using some of that content with one of your competitors?

Second, businesses should retain IPR over all data and results but share this unconditionally with the vendor. So if a firm pays to use a psychometric test, it should have the IPR over all the results and reports produced. However, since vendors use these data to produce norm groups and studies, organizations need to share the intellectual property with vendors. This is often done by granting a "perpetual, royalty-free license to use data in an anonymous form for the purpose of norm generation and research." The principle is that both parties should be free to use the data for their respective purposes. Sometimes vendors do not want to provide data to a business, for example, when an assessment has been part of a developmental process. But in our view, as long as the data are kept securely within the business's central measurement team and confidentiality is maintained, if the business has paid for the data, it should be able to use it.

Intellectual property, then, is an important issue. At stake is a company's freedom to choose to work with another vendor or walk away if a vendor does not do a good job. This freedom is so fundamental that we have one overarching piece of advice: if a vendor insists on retaining IPR over something new that you pay it to design or if it is unwilling to share IPR on data with you, find another vendor that will. No debate, no exceptions.

Total Price. In principle, this ought to be easier than the intellectual property issue, but it is not always. Businesses need to be clear not only on the upfront costs of using a measure but also on the total costs across the lifetime of a contract. Obviously, at the beginning, it is often not certain how much a measure will be used. But the extra add-on costs that can emerge need to be specified in advance. For example, project management fees increasingly seem to be viewed as an add-on. We experienced one vendor showing these costs in a brief comment in small print at the bottom of its proposal: "A 14 percent project management fee will be added to all costs." It claimed that it had separated out the cost to make the charges easier to understand, but we were not convinced by this, and indeed remain unconvinced.

Other common add-on costs are things like training end users to use reports (which some vendors may insist on) and training staff to use test administration systems (which may be necessary). With psychometrics, be aware of any test development that may be required, such as additional translations or the development of norm groups specific to your business. Finally, some vendors charge extra for attending annual or quarterly review meetings, although we recommend that you do not accept any such charges.

The key here is to be aware of potential additional costs and that some vendors are more forthcoming and clearer in presenting them than others.

Travel Claims. This is not usually a contentious issue, but it is one to be aware of. The idea here is that vendors should not charge for the time it takes them to travel to and from any location to complete work for a business if that travel lasts less than a certain number of hours (door-to-door). There are regional variations in what this number is, but it is usually between two and four hours. When travel takes longer than this, the total time spent traveling is typically charged at 50 percent of consultants' normal day rate.

Targets, Performance Indicators, and Penalty Clauses. All contracts should lay out clear targets, performance indicators, and penalties. Organizations that do this well tend to report higher levels of vendor performance and lower levels of opportunistic behavior from vendors. The bit that is often missed is the penalty clauses. Yet they are essential, since they set the boundaries of acceptable performance. Bear in mind, though, that this is a two-way street. Vendors may well want to place penalty clauses of their own, and for the most part, we support this. Contracts, after all, need to be fair to all parties.

Termination Clauses. Last, but by no means least, there should be no penalty if a business terminates a contract. Sometimes a vendor offers a reduced setup or design fee to attract businesses, but it compensates for this by applying higher fees per assessment or by assuming that it will receive a certain amount of business. In these situations, it might want a termination clause that ties businesses in for a certain period and thus gives the vendor a chance to recoup its setup costs. In our experience, it is better to pay a higher setup fee and be free to walk away if thing go wrong than to choose lower setup costs at the expense of being tied to a vendor.

How to Manage Vendors

When it comes to managing measurement vendors, all of the usual guidelines apply, including being clear about expectations and communicating openly. Make sure, then, that there are regular review meetings and, where possible, foster a spirit of partnership. Nevertheless, there are a number of issues that are particularly relevant for measurement vendors.

Onboard Vendors. Without an onboarding plan, it can be difficult to ensure that vendors have the necessary level of understanding about the business and its culture to develop and deliver effective solutions. With methods such as assessment centers and individual psychological assessment, for example, assessors need to understand the business if they are to make accurate judgments about individuals' level of fit with it.

If you are using these methods, it is important to arrange an induction to the business for the vendor's team of assessors. The introduction should familiarize them with the company's strategy and culture and advise on the types of people who tend to do well in the business: that is, those who tend to fit in well with the culture, perform well, and be promoted. It is also important to arrange a conversation between the assessor and the manager or hiring manager of an individual being assessed. The manager can then advise on the challenges the individual will face in the role and the stakeholders he or she will have to work and interact with.

Obviously, with measures such as psychometrics, these steps are not so relevant. Yet for processes in which an assessor is making judgments, they can be critical. So we are continually surprised by the lack of attention paid to them. Many businesses seem to assume that vendors have business knowledge and therefore skip this step. Yet by doing so, they risk limiting the effectiveness of any measures, since without these briefings, assessors cannot accurately measure fit.

Evaluate Vendors. In early 2011, the Romanian parliament sat down to discuss a controversial new law: that Romanian witches and fortune-tellers making predictions about the future should be penalized if their predictions did not come true. At the risk of being cursed, we think this is a good idea, and not just for witches. Measurement vendors are effectively making predictions about the future—about who is likely to succeed and who is not. Yet businesses all too often purchase measures without subsequently checking if the measures genuinely are predictive. Indeed, we never cease to be amazed by the number of firms that speak highly of their vendors but have no hard, internally produced data to back this up. Since firms invariably go on to purchase more measures, this is extraordinarily bad business.

This is why in chapter 6 we described the need to evaluate the impact of measures as one of the four foundations of making measurement work. And as we noted there, this is more than about simply checking whether measures work after the fact.

Measuring effectiveness is a key element of tailoring tools to businesses' specific needs, and if this not done, organizations are limiting the effectiveness of measures.

Leverage Market Forces in Managing Suppliers. Larger organizations often use multiple vendors, yet few have an active plan to leverage the market forces that can be created by having more than one vendor. This is a lost opportunity, since research shows that the market forces created by competition between vendors can result in improved service levels and reduced costs.[1] There are three things in particular that businesses can do here: do not let the vendor pool grow too large, measure vendors' performance, and make these performance data widely available.

For example, when setting up an individual psychological assessment process for new senior-level staff across a large multinational energy firm, we realized that the sheer number of locations meant that we were going to need more than one vendor. We therefore launched what we called a guided calibrated market. We selected three vendors and agreed on a common format for the IPAs, a common process for scheduling them, and common, standardized reports. We also used standardized contracts to ensure that the terms and conditions were the same for each vendor. The only element that differed between them was the price. We then gave the various business units the choice of which of the three vendors to select. We brought the vendors together regularly to calibrate judgments and tracked their rating tendencies statistically. We also measured their performance along a number of dimensions and made this information available to the business units on an ongoing basis. Finally, at the end of every year, we evaluated whether to retain the vendors or replace some or all of them. The business loved having the choice, and we are certain that we achieved a better-quality process and lower costs by adopting this approach.

Beware Closed Systems. One way organizations seek to control the quality of vendors across diverse business units is to use preferred supplier lists. Although these lists have their benefits, it is critical to have a mechanism for promoting new suppliers onto the list and removing existing suppliers from it. Without such a mechanism, businesses' ability to apply market pressures to vendors will be limited.

Invest in Vendor Management Skills

Research shows that effective vendor management is the single most significant factor within a company's control for ensuring successful outcomes with vendors.[2] Yet many companies appear to assume that employees already have these skills. Do not make this assumption. Given the large amounts that some businesses spend with vendors, investing in vendor management skills is vital.

On Track for Successful Implementation

In the previous three chapters, we looked at the challenges and opportunities in implementing measurement. We laid out four clear foundations for making measurement work and ensure that it has the impact it should. We looked at how to make the most of results and turn all the talent data produced into talent intelligence, capable of doing more than merely informing individual people decisions. And now, in this chapter, we have looked at how to source the expertise needed to do all this. We have considered how to select, contract with, and manage vendors and how firms that employ internal experts can make sure they have the right kind of expertise in the right places to make a real difference.

Implementation has long been the forgotten side of measurement. All the headlines seem to have gone to the selection of products and vendors. And when implementation has been considered, it has tended to be in terms of the project management or communications involved. These are important, and we do not want to downplay them. But measurement is not the same as any other business process. It has quirks and idiosyncrasies that require special attention, and if you ignore them, you risk undermining the effectiveness and value of measures.

More than anything else, it was this neglected side of measurement that drove us to write this book. If you take nothing else away, we hope you will have acquired increased awareness of these implementation issues, a sense that you now know what to do about them, and a belief that you can do it.

9

MAKING MEASUREMENT WORK

In this book, we have explored and explained some of the intricacies of producing good talent intelligence. We have acknowledged the complexities of measuring talent, while at the same time showing how, with a little understanding of it, many of the solutions can be simple. And we have argued that if talent measurement is to work, it cannot be taken for granted or treated as a peripheral activity.

All companies use measurement to some extent, even if it is only in the form of unstructured, informal interviews. It provides them with some much-needed help, grounding their people decisions in evidence. Done well, measurement can enhance selection processes, resulting in improved job performance, accelerated time to full productivity, and reduced failure rates and employee turnover.

Yet in many, if not most, businesses, measurement is not working well and is not having the impact it should. Expertise and understanding are often lacking. Either the wrong thing is measured, or it is assessed using the wrong kind of tool, or it is used in the wrong way. Other times, the outputs—the results of measurement—are used in only a limited way.

This book, then, was born in part out of frustration that, time and again, we found ourselves wondering how businesses can fail to get right something that is so fundamental. It *is* fundamental too. It may not be HR's headline act, but it underpins much, if not most, talent management and development activity. But it can only do this if it works.

Compounding our frustration is the knowledge that the solutions required to make measurement work are not difficult or expensive. They are mostly a matter of knowing what to do and having the will to do it. It is in businesses' power and remit to make measurement work. It is an opportunity waiting to be seized. And given the rising talent challenges facing businesses, it is an opportunity that they must seize.

Four Steps to Making Measurement Work

In the preceding chapters, we have laid out a plan for what organizations need to do. We have presented the issues in what we hope is a logical format. We focused first on how to make sure that the right things are measured, then on which tools to use, and, finally, on how to implement measurement and extract the maximum value from the information gathered.

We are aware, though, that businesses may not have the luxury of approaching things in this order. They may already have measurement processes up and running and perhaps neither the resources nor the political leeway to change much. So in these situations, how should businesses proceed?

Step 1: Become an Educated Consumer

The first step for any business is to become an educated consumer. This is not about being an expert or having access to expertise. It is about asking the right questions and looking at the right issues. It is about being able to tell a good tool from a poor one and about being able to see through the next measurement fad or emotional intelligence–type myth. More specifically:

- Use the guide in chapters 2 and 3 to better understand what factors or signs of talent you need to measure, not forgetting incremental validity. Currently businesses rely largely on their suppliers to understand their demand for them. This has to change.

- Read chapter 4 to help you understand what kinds of tools you need to measure with.

- Consult the guides to understanding validity in chapter 5 and the appendix to help define what questions to ask about tools in order to ascertain whether they can work as you need them to. And remember: do not simply accept what you are told; be aware of reporting bias, and ask to see evidence that measures and methods do work.

Step 2: Put the First Foundations in Place

In chapter 6, we described four foundations for making measurement work, but if your room to maneuver is limited, focus only on the first three. They are relatively easy to implement and can help provide the data you need to build a business case for acting on the fourth one. Even if you have not done these things to date, draw a line and start now:

- Collect the data centrally. You do not need a fancy system; a simple spreadsheet will do. And remember to collect not only measurement results but also other essential information, such as performance scores and employee turnover.

- Use common data points to assess the same things across the company wherever possible.

- Check the impact of measures. Make sure that they work, are predictive of success, and are having the impact they should. We have come across too many businesses that have been using the same tools for a long time but are unable to answer the basic question: "How do you know they work?" This is plainly bad business—especially because if you are collecting results and performance scores, conducting an evaluation is simple and quick to do.

Talent measurement processes and tools are precision instruments that require fine-tuning and should not be expected to work perfectly straight out of the box. This means using both the results of measurement and the evaluation of how the measures work to adjust, hone, and improve them.

Step 3: Ensure Proper Use

There is no getting around it: sooner or later, the fourth foundation from chapter 6—ensuring proper use—needs to be laid. We have seen businesses that proudly speak of their long history of using talent measures but that have done almost nothing to ensure that the results of talent measures are used properly. So to ensure proper use:

- If you are starting a new measurement process or making changes to an existing one, start small, perhaps with a trial in one part of the business. Keep it simple, and do it right. It is better to use fewer measurement methods and to use them effectively than to use many of them poorly.

- Get the interview right. It is the most basic and frequently used measurement method. Avoid generic interview systems and fully structured interviews if you can, and create a simple and clear process (see chapter 7).

- Focus on how people decisions are made, provide clear guidelines for how to use measurement results, and create accountability for the quality of these decisions and how measures are used. Track and follow up on hiring and promotion decisions, and review the original decision (see chapter 7).

- Use the Three Cs model to help the business think about some of the complexities involved. Make it second nature for managers to question, for each quality or ability, the contexts, consequences, and caveats (see chapter 3). Introduce this terminology on all assessment reports.

- Make the move from talent identification to talent matching. Focus less on whether people are good and more on what they are good at. And make sure that the concept of fit is broad. It is not only about person-job fit but also about person-organization fit, person-team fit, and person-manager fit (see chapter 3). Make fit a core part of recruitment and promotion processes. It does not have to be complicated. Indeed, it is better to do it simply than not at all.

Step 4: Do More Than Merely Measure

The final step is about using measurement results to do more than merely inform individual people decisions and development. It is about using them to turn your administrative talent data into genuine talent intelligence.

Link results to other people data and use this information to guide other people processes. Turn your talent data into talent intelligence. Information is the currency of understanding, and harnessing measurement data can help businesses improve their bottom-line performance.

Measure more than one type of performance. Drive and enable the market to develop better measures for your better business.

Transforming the Market

Taking these four steps will do nothing short of transforming the value and impact of talent measurement in your business. And in doing so, it will also give your talent management and development processes a fighting chance of success in the challenges they face.

Moreover, if enough businesses take these steps, it will do more than just make measurement work on an individual basis: it will transform the market. And the market does need transforming. There are some brilliant tools and wonderful vendors, but also a lot of vendors who promote measures without having any validity data or—perhaps worse—using misrepresented, overly positive data. Only businesses, the consumers of measurement, can change this.

With a few noticeable exceptions, tools are generally no more able to predict success today than they were thirty years ago. The predictive power of measurement has by and large stalled. Vendors continually advertise new and improved tests. Yet we are frankly bored of announcements that a revolution in measurement is on its way. Building a bigger database or combining existing tools into a new online format does not count as a revolution.

Again, only businesses can change this. Vendors rely on organizations to help them address the criterion issue by measuring more than just overall performance and to help them use the results of measurement to improve tools. Businesses are going to have to take the lead in this; real change will come only when they do.

Companies may have been slow to act, but the growing talent challenges and the need for talent intelligence provide a compelling reason to do so now. Big or small, global or local, organizations need to get this right. The good news is that they can. Measurement itself may be a complex task, but making it work need not be.

Appendix: Frequently Asked Questions

This appendix contains a collection of specific, practical questions that we are commonly asked. There are some big and important issues here, such as how to check whether a competency framework is suitable for assessment and whether it is possible to measure integrity. For the most part, you do not need to have read the rest of the book to understand the answers. But we suggest you look at the definition of *validity* in chapter 2 if you have not read it yet. The questions we address are:

1. Why are there so many different types of validity?
2. How can I tell if a competency framework is suitable for assessing people?
3. What are the best predictors of success in international assignments?
4. Is it possible to measure integrity?
5. Is drug testing useful?
6. What kind of intelligence test should I use?
7. There are so many different personality tests. Which one is best?
8. Should I be worried about the effect of faking on personality test results?
9. What type of situational judgment test should I use to assess training needs?
10. Four quick questions about 360-degree feedback.

11. What should I look for when choosing a vendor to provide individual psychological assessments?

If you would like to see more further frequently asked questions and answers or pose a question of your own, you can do so at our online blog (www.measuringtalent.com).

1. Why Are There So Many Different Types of Validity?

For the most part, we have tried to avoid using technical language in this book. This is particularly true when it comes to the issue of validity. To keep things simple, we have mainly discussed validity as if it is just one thing: the ability to predict future workplace success. Yet this is only one very specific gauge of validity, and there are others that it might be useful to know about.

We hinted at this in chapter 2 when we described two basic quality checks that vendors should make when developing measures: whether the measure is accurate in its measurements and whether it can help predict things like certain behaviors, events, or the chance that someone will succeed at something.

These checks roughly equate to two big concepts in the world of validity. Accuracy is broadly equivalent to what psychologists call *construct validity*: the degree to which a measure genuinely assesses what it says it does. So with an intelligence test, does it really measure intelligence? Validity is important because many of the elements that we try to look at in talent measurement are quite subjective. Ask three people for a broad definition of *adaptability*, and you will get roughly the same answer. But ask them to specify exactly what adaptability involves and what the best questions to evaluate it are, and you are likely to obtain three entirely different answers.

To help ensure that methods and tools do indeed measure what they are supposed to, vendors often look at three specific things:

- They check whether the content of a test, such as the questions it asks, is relevant to and capable of capturing what they are trying to measure. For example, with a test of ambition, they need to ensure the questions it contains are indeed about ambition and capture all the different types of ambition. A test developer will thus often give a list of potential questions to a group of experts and ask them to rate which ones are most relevant. The developer can then use statistical techniques to work out which questions are best. This is called *content validity*.

- Vendors can also check the degree to which results on a measure are similar to things that they should be similar to. So if they are developing an intelligence test, they will check whether people who score highly on their test also score highly on other intelligence tests. This is called *convergent validity*.

- They can check whether results on a test are different (or diverge) from things that it is thought they should be different from. For example, do people who score well on tests of integrity have a low incidence of criminal behavior? This is called *divergent validity*.

The ability of tests to predict certain things, meanwhile, is what psychologists call *criterion validity*. The thing we usually try to predict is performance, but it can be pretty much anything—from turnover and absenteeism to productivity and promotion. There are three types of criterion validity:

- *Concurrent validity* is whether a measure can predict something else that is measured at around the same time—for example, whether a score on an intelligence test that you take today predicts the performance rating that you receive in this year's appraisal. This is the most common type of criterion validity that is measured.

- *Predictive validity* is what we have focused on in this book. It is how well a measure can predict something in the future, such as performance ratings—so whether a score on an intelligence test that you take today predicts the performance rating that you receive in next year's appraisal.

- *Incremental validity*, as described in chapter 2, is the amount of criterion validity that a measure provides over and above another measure—in other words, how much additional information or validity it provides you with over whatever other measures you are using.

We have focused on predictive criterion validity in this book because it is what businesses tend to be most interested in. But it is worth being aware of the other types of validity, and we have two specific recommendations here:

- *Ask vendors about construct validity.* One interesting and useful question to ask a vendor is how it knows that its measures have construct validity. The answer can tell you a lot about both the test and the vendor and its approach to making sure that its measures are valid.

- *Distinguish between concurrent and predictive validity.* Most measures are validated using concurrent validity. But it is rare to hear a vendor use this phrase, and we have frequently heard vendors say "predictive validity" when they mean "concurrent validity." If you are told that a measure has been shown to predict performance, check whether this means performance now or in the future. Concurrent validity can be useful, but predictive validity is the higher bar to set when evaluating measures.

Finally, there are a few other validity phrases that you will sometimes hear mentioned:

- *Face validity* is whether something appears to measure what it says it does. You often hear this talked about in relation to participant reactions to various measurement methods.
- *Faith validity* is the tendency to become attached to particular tests or vendors that you are familiar with, at the expense of objectively considering what works best.[1]
- *Mythical validity* is how much validity people believe a test has (regardless of the reality).[2]

2. How Can I Tell If a Competency Framework Is Suitable for Assessing People?

To check whether a framework is suitable for assessing people, we suggest six simple criteria.

1.   *Whenever possible, competencies should be personal to a business.* As we saw in chapter 3, assessments that take into account the specific circumstances and needs of a business are likely to be more accurate in predicting individuals' success in those environments. So the more specific and personal that a competency framework is to your company, business unit, or team, the more effective it is likely to be for measuring talent. This is why we prefer not to use generic competency frameworks owned by vendors. For small businesses that do not have the time, resources, or inclination to develop a framework, using a generic model is better than not using anything. But as a rule, good business-specific competency frameworks are likely to be more useful and to lead to better people decisions than generic ones.

2.   *Competencies must help distinguish between the good and the great.* Businesses often put a lot of thought into which

competencies are most relevant to them. Yet they tend to think a lot less about how effective they are at differentiating among people. And to be useful, competencies need to be able to do this. For example, honesty is definitely desirable, but it does not make a good measurement competency. It is common for over 95 percent of employees to be rated highly on it, so it does not help you to identify different types of talent. For similar reasons, we would advise against the current vogue of having a "values" framework. From a measurement point of view, it tends not to add value.

3. *There should not be too many competencies.* Some vendors use frameworks with fifty or more competencies. For the vendors this can be useful, but for organizations, it is too many. Indeed, in most businesses, it is unrealistic to ask managers to rate any more than a handful of things. This is probably just as well, for research suggests that even trained assessors cannot accurately evaluate more than four or so things at one time. We therefore recommend having no more than six to eight competencies.

4. *The framework must have a good life expectancy.* Data points need to be consistent not only over business units but also over time. To learn about talent trends, you need to use the same framework over a number of years. One phenomenon that can prove challenging is when the CEO champions a particular competency. The risk here is that when the CEO changes, so does the framework. So although competencies need to reflect current business challenges, they also need to enable continuity of data.

5. *Detail is necessary, but not too much.* Typically each competency in a framework is accompanied by "behavioral indicators"—examples of what the competency is all about and what "good" looks like. This kind of detail is important to make sure that competencies are rated accurately and

consistently. However, it is critical not to have too much detail. We saw one business whose framework was accompanied by a 120-page book. This described in detail, for each competency and level of employee, the behaviors required for particular ratings to be given. From a purist's perspective, this was good practice. Yet from an operational point of view, it was unworkable. Managers do not have time for this level of detail, so keep it simple. For each competency, have a few examples of both good and poor practice. While you may need different indicators for senior- and lower-level roles, you should not need separate ones for each individual level. Some might argue that this lacks rigor and will lead to inaccurate data. Yet managers are more likely to rate accurately using a few simple indicators than when ignoring a hundred-page document.

6. *Global frameworks need to be globally applicable.* Global companies need to assess competencies across different cultures. The challenge here is whether to assess people in different cultures against local standards or to assess everyone everywhere against common standards. One driver for this is that what is considered good leadership can vary by culture. One option is to use different frameworks in each country. But since the differences among countries tend to be small, we generally advise against this. However, where bigger differences do exist is that some competencies look very different in different cultures. To take a classic example, being able to influence effectively involves different behaviors in the United States than in Japan. To accommodate this, we recommend using slightly different behavior indicators in different countries. This still allows you to collect data on common competencies while also ensuring cross-cultural fairness.

3. What Are the Best Predictors of Success in International Assignments?

International assignments are a common developmental tool and are seen as an opportunity for growth. But they can also be challenging. There is much debate about how high failure rates really are, but almost everyone agrees that careful selection is necessary. So what should you look for?

To begin, there are some specialist tools on the market. For the most part, they measure intercultural competence: the ability to engage with, understand, and operate within other cultures. This certainly sounds useful, and the developers of these tests invariably describe them as valid. Yet you do need to be careful here. What they usually mean by "valid" is that the tests are accurate: they genuinely measure intercultural competence. However, solid evidence that these tools are able to predict success in assignments is largely lacking.

What are the options, then? Prior international experience appears to help, but its ability to predict success is very low. Flexibility and adaptability appear to be more predictive of success, although the research on them is limited.[3] The role of the Big Five personality factors has been more often studied (see chapter 2). For the most part, the ability of these factors to predict assignee success has been fairly low. For example, the validities found for conscientiousness are around 0.17, and for emotional stability around 0.10.[4] However, one aspect of personality that does appear promising in predicting success is relational skills— the ability to build relationships. A combination of extraversion and agreeableness has thus been shown to have predictive validities of around 0.32.[5] The idea is that the more able people are to build relationships, the more opportunities they will have to engage with and adjust to different cultures. For similar reasons, language skills are also often touted as important. Yet with validities of only around 0.2, they appear to be less predictive than relational skills.

A number of studies have now shown that even more important than the assignee's personal qualities can be the family factor. This is the role of the family, and in particular the assignee's partner, in making the move a success. The burden on the partner is often considerable, and when this aspect of a move fails, the whole assignment can fail too.[6] Indeed, some studies have suggested that this is the single most important factor in determining success, or at least in avoiding failure.[7] Many companies seem to focus only on the assignee. But given the research, we recommend involving the whole family in the selection process at the earliest possible stage.

Finally, remember that in looking at personality and the family factor, you should not overlook some of the standard factors used for predicting job success. Aspects like job knowledge and intelligence are just as important for overseas roles as they are for home country ones. To summarize, our recommendation for selecting international assignees is to focus on these:

- The family factor
- Relational skills
- Job knowledge
- Intelligence
- Adaptability

4. Is It Possible to Measure Integrity?

Tests of people's integrity are nothing new, but they have become popular only in the past twenty years. The trigger for the increased interest in these tests was the introduction of regulations in the United States in 1988 that restricted the use of polygraphs. The annual cost to firms of some employee behaviors such as theft can be considerable, so there was a demand for other ways to identify people who were likely to engage in these behaviors. Enter integrity tests.

The use of these tests was at first mainly limited to measuring the likelihood of theft. Over the years, though, they have begun to be used to predict a broader range of counterproductive work behaviors (CWBs). These include not only theft but also absenteeism, drug use, unsafe behavior, and violence or bullying.

The vast majority of integrity tests available on the market today are psychometrics, and there are two main types.[8] *Overt* measures do not disguise their purpose: they ask direct questions about the extent to which people have engaged in illegal or unacceptable behaviors. *Covert* measures, by contrast, do disguise their purpose and are usually based on standard personality tests. The idea behind these tests is that people with certain types of personality are more likely to engage in CWBs.

Do they work? There is evidence to suggest that they can, with validities of up to 0.4 being reported for their ability to predict some CWBs. This means that at their best, they are more able to predict CWBs than personality tests are able to predict job performance. Some researchers have questioned whether overt tests of integrity in particular can work, since they are easy to fake. But others have argued that regardless of whether some people fake their responses, these tests can still predict CWBs in many people. They have also been shown to be able to reduce incidences of behaviors such as theft in real work situations. So there is some evidence to suggest that in some scenarios, integrity tests can indeed be effective and add value. However, there are some big caveats here.

First, the ability of integrity tests to predict CWBs varies according to the test you use and the specific CWBs you try to predict. For example, some overt tests have been shown to be good predictors of theft, with validities of up to 0.36 reported. Yet overt tests tend to be fairly poor predictors of absenteeism, with validities of around 0.14.[9] Similarly, the personality dimension of conscientiousness has been shown to be quite predictive of CWBs aimed at the organization, such as theft. Yet it is far less effective at predicting CWBs aimed at individuals, such as antisocial behavior.[10]

Second, the research that has been done to date on integrity tests mainly relates to moderate- to low-level jobs. There is a notable lack of evidence that these tests can be successfully used with more senior roles and more complex types of CWBs. For instance, we recently advised a financial trading business against using an integrity test as part of its selection processes for hiring traders. There is simply not enough evidence that they work in these situations.

Third, there can be some practical issues with integrity tests, such as whether and how to exclude candidates purely on the basis of their integrity test results. The problem here is that all integrity tests will inevitably produce a number of false positives. These are people who do poorly on the test but do not subsequently go on to demonstrate any CWBs. In fact, they can go on to be model corporate citizens. For this reason, integrity tests are far better used as an indicator for further investigation (for example, in an interview) than as a pass-or-fail type of test.

Finally, one aspect to be wary of when deciding whether to use integrity tests is reporting bias. Validity studies conducted by vendors selling integrity tests tend to report much higher validities than independent research into the efficacy of these tests.[11] So what does all this mean for companies considering using integrity tests? We have three recommendations:

- *Be clear about which specific CWBs you want to measure.* This is important so that you can make sure that the test you use is capable of doing precisely what you need it to do. In addition, an integrity test is usually more able to predict a specific CWB than a general tendency toward CWBs overall. Covert, personality-based integrity tests, for example, have been shown to predict CWBs overall with a fairly low validity of around 0.22.[12] Yet when we look at the ability of specific personality dimensions to predict particular CWBs, we can get validities of up to 0.36.[13] When considering which test to use, then, do not just ask, "How valid is it?" Ask, "How able is it to predict this specific behavior?"

- *Do not use integrity tests to try to measure complex CWBs in senior-level people.* There is not sufficient evidence that they can do this effectively, and more senior-level people tend to have less patience with having their integrity measured.

- *Ask integrity test vendors if there has been any independent research into the validity of their tests.* Also, check some of the independent review sources, such as the Buros Institute (see chapter 5).

One final thing to bear in mind is that the causes of CWBs do not lie only within individuals. Contextual factors have also been shown to be important and, sometimes, to be even better predictors of CWBs than traditional integrity tests. For example, the greater the level of fit there is between a role and an individual's career goals, the less chance there is he or she will engage in CWBs.[14] And low levels of job satisfaction have been shown to be more related to CWBs than many tests of integrity.[15] More research is required, but as with trying to predict job performance, the answer is unlikely to lie only within individuals.

5. Is Drug Testing Useful?

The answer depends on what you are trying to achieve. If you are trying to assess who takes illegal drugs (or at least fails to hide the fact that they do), then yes it can be. If you are trying to predict absence, then again, yes it can be. But if you are trying to predict accident proneness, then it is probably not useful. And if you are trying to predict performance, it is almost definitely not.[16]

6. What Kind of Intelligence Test Should I Use?

There are two main ways of thinking about the different types of intelligent tests. The first way, which you may already be familiar with, is according to the types of questions asked. The most common forms of questions are numerical, verbal (which test someone's ability to work with language), logical, diagrammatic, and mechanical. Some tests use only one type of question; others use two or three different types. No one type is best.

As for which to use, our recommendation would be to choose the two or three that are most relevant to the roles you are assessing. We say at least two because although in general people's scores on one type of question predict their scores on the other types, this is not always so. Sometimes people do excellently on, say, a verbal test but poorly on a mathematical one. One additional thing to bear in mind here is that the amount of adverse impact created by intelligence tests sometimes differs for each type of question. This is particularly so for people of different genders and ages. Men, for example, tend to do better on numerical and diagrammatic questions, whereas women tend to do better on verbal ones. And our ability to do verbal tests seems to decline more slowly with age than our ability to do other types of tests.[17]

The second way to think about what type of test you need is to consider whether it is a *speeded* test or a *power* test. One of the best examples of a speeded test is the Wonderlic. This is a well-known US test that in its classic form requires people to answer fifty-two verbal and numerical questions in 12 minutes. This means, on average, they need to answer one question every 13.85 seconds. That's speeded. At the other end of the scale are power tests. They typically last 20 to 40 minutes and ask only one type of question. Each question requires more thought and takes longer to answer than in a speeded test. As for which you should use, we again recommend thinking about the requirements of the role. Is quick thinking an important part of it? And again, adverse impact can be an issue, since there are reports that speeded tests can show greater levels of adverse impact.

Finally, there are some tests available that measure very specific aspects of thinking. One of the best known is the Vienna Test System, which involves over thirty separate tests. It can measure things like coordination and the ability to divide or sustain attention or to switch between tasks. They are mostly used for specialized roles, such as for pilots, but we have also seen them used with financial traders.

7. There Are So Many Different Personality Tests. Which One Is Best?

The obvious place to start is with validity. Unfortunately, though, there are few studies that directly compare the validity of different personality tests. One notable, albeit not independent, exception is Saville Consulting's recent Project Epsom, which compared the validity of four tests on a group of three hundred people and is freely available on the Internet.[18] In addition, as we described in chapter 5, the Buros Institute's test reviews can be a valuable resource, although it reviews tools individually rather than comparing different ones.

So validity is clearly one thing you need to consider. But there are three other things as well. First, check whether a personality test measures what you need it to. You may, for example, be particularly interested in measuring assertiveness, in which case you need a test that does just this. Some tests measure the Big Five personality dimensions, but many tests measure other aspects of personality, so you do have a choice. Remember, though, that even if you are interested in only one thing, you will need a test that measures multiple aspects of personality. For example, you may be trying to identify assertive people, but it is also useful to know how empathic or socially sensitive they are. After all, being assertive while also being sensitive to others is one thing; being both assertive and insensitive is quite another.

To make their tests more obviously relevant to a business and easier to use, some vendors offer to back-end their test onto your competency framework. This involves aligning their test to the different competencies of your framework and then presenting individuals' results as scores for each of the areas. However, you should do this only if there is a close alignment between the elements that a test measures and your competency framework. All too often we have seen businesses and vendors stretching reality and saying that there is alignment when there is not. And when this happens, the results that you obtain can mislead. Having a test that is accurate but less easy to use can present problems. But having one that is easy to use but inaccurate or misleading is pointless. Personality tests are designed to measure certain things, and there is only so much you can change about them.

Second, you need to look at the outputs available—the type of report that the tests provide. Ideally, you are looking for one that interprets scores for you in easy language that every manager will understand but does not provide too much detail. Our general rule is that a paragraph for each score is fine; a page is too much. Importantly, check to see whether the test has the capacity to evaluate fit with job requirements and business culture. Finally, some reports also provide suggestions for interview questions based on the results of the test. Yet in our experience, these questions tend to be basic and not very effective or useful. So unless your interviewers are particularly inexperienced, we would avoid these "interview" reports.

Finally, you need to think about whether you want a normative test or an ipsative one. The most common type of psychometric is a normative test: typically people rate aspects of their behavior or personality in response to certain questions. At the end, scores are calculated by adding up the responses and, importantly, are compared to a comparison norm group. Normative tests, then, allow you to compare individuals.

The second main type of test, ipsative or forced choice, is very different. People have to choose between different statements: for example, "Which word describes you best: assertive or fun-loving?" After a sufficient number of choices have been made, the test uses some clever mathematics to produce overall scores. Some of the best-known personality tests, including the MBTI, are ipsative.

There are lengthy debates about which type is better, and some providers have tried to produce tests that are a bit of both. The debate continues, but as a general rule, if you want to be able to compare the results of different people (such as in some recruitment situations), you should use only normative tests. Ipsative tests are not designed to do this, so if you try to compare the results of people using them, you will get some strange, invalid, and unreliable results. Knowing what you need to use the test for is important.

8. Should I Be Worried About the Effect of Faking on Personality Test Results?

Consciously or unconsciously, the vast majority of people try to present themselves in a good way when they are being assessed. With measurement methods in which there is some human contact, such as interviews, assessment centers, and individual psychological assessments, businesses tend to worry less about the impact of faking. This is presumably because they assume that assessors can see through any faking or impression management. Yet with indirect methods such as personality tests, we often hear managers say they are worried that faking could reduce the effectiveness of the tests, since people may appear to be different from how they really are.

The response of some researchers and vendors is that scores on personality tests still predict performance, regardless of whether the results have been achieved through honest answers or faking. Strictly speaking, this is true. But whether you should still be worried depends on the situation in which you are using the personality tests.

If you are using them to assess and sift a large number of candidates, then the researchers are probably right. This is because although a few fakers may slip through, the results will generally still be predictive of performance. However, in selection situations that do not involve large numbers of people, faking may be more of an issue. We thus recommend always talking through the test results with candidates so you have a chance to get a sense of whether the results are accurate.

9. What Type of Situational Judgment Test Should I Use to Assess Training Needs?

We have already mentioned the two basic types of situational judgment test: those that ask knowledge-based questions (what the correct answer is) and those that ask behavioral tendency questions (how people typically act). Each has its pros and cons, and both can be effective (see chapter 2).

One clear preference that we have is to use tests that also allow you to assess an individual's level of confidence in her or his answer to each question. The advantage of this is that it allows you to distinguish among four groups of people, each with a different level of training need:

- Those who get the correct answer and are confident about it. These people just need to be told they got it right.

- Those who get the correct answer but are not confident about it. These people probably guessed a bit and need to be told that they got it right, plus maybe reminded of some of the reasons it was the correct answer.

- Those who get the wrong answer and are not confident about it. Again, these people probably guessed and need to be told what the correct answer is and why.

- Those who get the wrong answer but are confident about it. These are the people you need to target most. They need to be told why they were wrong and trained or educated in the correct response.

10. Four Quick Questions About 360-Degree Feedback

1. *Should we buy a generic off-the-shelf 360 or create our own?* Generally you should consider developing your own: it is not difficult and can be quick and cheap to do. However, there are two situations in which it does make sense to use a generic test. First, if you plan to use the test only a few times or with only a few people, investing in creating your own test is not likely to be justified. Second, if you plan to use the test quite often, the one scenario in which using generic tests can still be better is if your business does not have its own competency framework *and* you can find a generic test that assesses what you need it to.

2. *Do the people presenting individuals with their 360-degree feedback results always need training?* No. They will probably do a better job if they have received training, but it is rarely absolutely necessary. This is an important issue because the quality of the conversation that occurs when people receive their 360 report can play a major role in determining whether the feedback leads to any performance improvement. And if handled poorly, it is true that—like any other feedback or appraisal conversation—it can have a negative impact on the recipient. So training is generally preferable, and we strongly urge companies to think about the skills of the individuals running these feedback conversations. But it is not absolutely necessary. This is why we recommend that you do not use vendors that insist on training and "certifying" people to be able to run these feedback conversations: not everyone may need it.

3. *What is the ideal number of feedback givers for a 360?* The consensus is six to eight people, but it is important not to go

much beyond this number. You may receive more written comments, but the average ratings for each category of feedback giver can become meaningless. This is because if you combine the ratings of too many people, the result is a lot of average overall scores, with no real highs or lows.

4. *Whose ratings are the most predictive of success?* The common answer you will hear is that managers' ratings are the most accurate, followed by peers' and then direct reports'. Self-ratings and customer ratings do not appear to be very accurate. However, there are two caveats:

- Although peers' ratings can clearly be useful and accurate, there is a lot of variation in how valid they have been found to be. For example, when there is little opportunity to observe the day-to-day performance of the individual, ratings tend to be less valid. Likewise, when the 360 is part of an appraisal or selection process, ratings tend to be less valid. Moreover, in our experience, peer ratings tend to reflect how agreeable and liked an individual is as much as anything else.

- Direct reports' ratings tend to be a bit high and have been found to be unreliable at distinguishing between high and low performers. However, they have been found to be predictive of team effectiveness, and there are some managerial behaviors that direct reports are well positioned to rate, so their ratings should never be ignored.

11. What Should I Look for When Choosing a Vendor to Provide Individual Psychological Assessments?

We looked at how to choose, contract, and manage vendors in chapter 8. To choose one specifically to provide IPAs, we suggest you consider four criteria:

○ *Cost and coverage.* How much will the vendor charge, and does it have consultants in all the locations that you want to assess people in? If not, charges could rise rapidly with travel costs. There are also two less obvious issues you should look at here. First, can the vendor cover all the languages of your employees, even in your home locations? Wherever possible, people should be assessed in their first language, and you may well have foreign nationals working in your head office. Second, check whether the consultants in locations abroad are locals or expatriates. This is particularly an issue in Africa, the Middle East, and Asia-Pacific, where it is common for assessors to be individuals with little knowledge of the local culture.

○ *Quality of the assessors.* As we explained in chapter 4, individual psychological assessment can be accurate, but it is totally reliant on the quality of the assessor, so you need to check this. How do you tell if an assessor is good? Start by asking the vendor who its best assessors are and how it knows this. Good vendors should have some data to show you—and on something more than simply the level of experience of the assessors. The answer can be interesting since it can show you what the vendor values in its assessors and how it evaluates their performance. Next, ask to see the résumés of all the assessors who would do assessments for you. It is important here that you see the real bench strength of the vendor, not just its top people. You are looking for two things in assessors: their level of experience as an assessor and their level of real business experience. Ideally, you want assessors who have both.

○ *Quality of the outputs.* This refers to how much you like the written reports that the vendor provides. All vendors will be able to provide you with an anonymized sample report. You should be looking for a good balance of ratings and descriptive text. Typically they provide competency ratings. You should also look for ratings of fit and—in selection processes—recommendation ratings (for instance, "hire" or "do not hire"). Some vendors do not like to give clear recommendation ratings. They believe that such definite judgments can be unreliable and can undermine the hiring manager's ownership of the hiring decision. Although we respect this position and appreciate that these judgments are difficult, we expect them of managers and so expect an opinion from paid expert assessors, too. Moreover, we do not believe that recommendation ratings undermine managers' ownership of the final decision. If anything, they accentuate managers' accountability for these decisions.

In terms of the text, beware of simple statements such as, "He is a good manager." Instead, remember the Four Cs from chapter 3 and look for statements such as, "He is an effective manager in this way when . . . but less so when . . ." Read the concluding or summary section to see if it provides a clear description, and, finally, look at the "development needs" or "weaknesses" section. Here you are looking for three things: each issue should be clearly described, the relevance of the issue for performance must be made clear, and a suggestion should be given for how to improve in the area.

○   *Quality of the calibration.* This is the process that vendors use to make sure that their assessors all rate people against the same standards. It is how they check that when one assessor gives a rating of 5, it means the same as when their other assessors do so. This is an essential process because it is how vendors can minimize the impact of rating biases. We would expect at a minimum to hear two things: that all reports are read and checked by a second person, who will read all the reports that the vendor provides for you, and that the vendor monitors (and will provide you with) information on things such as each assessor's rating tendencies. This is to make sure that, for example, a particular assessor is not always a bit harder in his or her ratings. Finally, we have occasionally come across some vendors that have tried to levy an extra charge for such calibration. To us, this feels wrong. Call us old-fashioned, but we firmly believe that vendors should not be charging extra for assuring you of the quality of their work.

Notes

Chapter One

1. Chambers, E. G., Foulton, M., Handfield-Jones, H., Hankin, S. M., & Michaels III, E. G. (1998). The war for talent. *McKinsey Quarterly*, 3, 44–57.
2. Boatman, J., & Wellins, R. S. (2011). *Global leadership forecast*. Pittsburgh, PA: Development Dimensions International; Bersin & Associates. (2011). *TalentWatch Q1 2011—global growth creates new war for talent*. Oakland, CA: Bersin & Associates.
3. Chartered Institute of Personnel and Development. (2011). *Resourcing and talent planning*. Annual survey report. London: Author; Society of Human Resource Management. (2011). *The ongoing impact of the recession: Recruiting and skill gap*. Alexandria, VA: Author.
4. Chartered Institute of Personnel and Development. (2011).
5. Axelrod, E. L., Handfield-Jones, H., & Welsh, T. (2001). The war for talent, part two. *McKinsey Quarterly*, 2, 9–11; Huselid, M. A. (1995). The impact of human resource management practices on turnover, productivity, and corporate financial performance. *Academy of Management Journal*, 38(3), 635–872; Combs, J., Liu, Y., Hall, A., & Ketchen, D. (2006). How much do high-performance work practices matter? A meta-analysis of their effects on organizational performance. *Personnel Psychology*, 59, 501–528.
6. Watson Wyatt. (2002). *Linking human capital and shareholder value: Human capital index*. Fourth European survey report. London: Watson Wyatt Worldwide.
7. Lacey, A. T., & Wright, B. (2010). *Occupational employment projections to 2018*. Retrieved from http://www.bls.gov/opub/mlr/2009/11/art5full.pdf

8. Hansell, S. (2007, January 3). Google answer to filling jobs is an algorithm. *New York Times*.

9. Chartered Institute of Personnel and Development. (2011).

10. Boatman, J., & Wellins, R. S. (2011). *Global leadership forecast*. Pittsburgh, PA: Development Dimensions International.

11. Drucker, P. F. (1985, July-August). How to make people decisions. *Harvard Business Review*, 22–26.

12. Hogan, R. (2010). *How to defend personality measurement*. Tulsa, OK: Hogan Assessments.

13. Cohen, D. S. (2001). *Talent edge*. Ontario, Canada: Wiley.

14. Cohen. (2001).

15. Highhouse, S. (2008). Stubborn reliance on intuition and subjectivity in employee selection. *Industrial and Organizational Psychology*, *1*, 333–342.

16. Cook, M. (2009). *Personnel selection: Adding value through people* (5th ed.). Chichester, UK: Wiley; Schmidt, F. L., & Hunter, J. E. (1998). The validity and utility of selection methods in personnel psychology: Practical and theoretical implications of 85 years of research findings. *Psychological Bulletin*, *124*(2), 262–274.

17. Landis, D., Brousseau, K. R., & Johnson, P. N. (2011). *Pre-hiring assessment improves the executive talent pipeline*. Los Angeles, CA: Korn/Ferry Institute.

18. Rynes, S. L., Colbert, A. E., & Brown, K. G. (2002). HR professionals' beliefs about effective human resource practices. *Human Resource Management*, *41*(1), 149–174; Buckley, M. R., Ferris, G. R., Bernardin, H. J., & Harvey, M. G. (1998). The disconnect between the science and practice of management. *Business Horizons*, *41*(2), 31–38; Terpstra, D. E., & Rozell, E. J. (1998). Human resource executives' perceptions of academic research. *Journal of Business and Psychology*, *13*, 19–29.

19. Hogan, R. (2005). In defense of personality measurement: New wine for old whiners. *Human Performance*, *18*(4), 331–341.

20. Russell, C. J., Settoon, R. P., McGrath, R. N., Blanton, A. E., Kidwell, R. E., Lohrke, F. T., et al. (1994). Investigator characteristics as moderators of personnel selection research: A meta-analysis. *Journal of Applied Psychology*, *79*, 163–170.

21. McDaniel, M. A., Rothstein, H. R., & Whetzel, D. L. (2006). Publication BIAS: A case study of four test vendors. *Personnel Psychology, 59,* 927–953.

22. Spies, R. A., & Plake, B. S. (Eds.). (2005). *The sixteenth mental measurements yearbook.* Lincoln, NE: Buros Institute of Mental Measurements.

23. Hay Group. (n.d.). *Emotional and social intelligence for effective leadership.* Retrieved November 16, 2011, from http://www.haygroup .com/leadershipandtalentondemand/leadershipsolutions/develop ment-programs/emotional-leadership.aspx

24. Roulin, N., & Bangerter, A. (2012). Understanding the academic-practitioner gap for structured interviews: "Behavioral" interviews diffuse, "structured" interviews do not. *International Journal of Selection and Assessment, 20,* 149–158.

25. MacKinnon, R. A. (2010). *Assessment and talent management survey.* London: TalentQ.

26. Terpstra, D. E. (1996). The search for effective methods. *HR Focus, 73,* 16–17; Terpstra, D. E., & Rozell, E. J. (1997). Attitudes of practitioners in human resource management toward information from academic research. *Psychological Reports, 80,* 403–412.

27. Saville, P., MacIver, R., Kurz, R., & Hopton, T. (2008, January). *Project Epsom: How valid is your questionnaire?* Paper presented at the British Psychological Society Division of Occupational Psychology Conference, Stratford-upon-Avon.

28. Konig, C. J., Jöri, E., & Knüsel, P. (2011). The amazing diversity of thought: A qualitative study on how human resource practitioners perceive selection procedures. *Journal of Business and Psychology, 26*(4), 437–452.

29. Ryan, A. M., & Tippins, N. T. (2004). Attracting and selecting: What psychological research tells us. *Human Resource Management, 43*(4), 305–318.

30. Furnham, A., Dissou, G., Sloan, P., & Chamorro-Premuzic, T. (2008). Personality and intelligence in business people: A study of two personality and two intelligence measures. *Journal of Business Psychology, 22,* 99–109.

31. Scroggins, W. A., Benson, P. G., Cross, C., & Gilbreath, B. (2008). Reactions to selection methods: An international comparison. *International Journal of Management, 25*(2), 203–216.

Chapter Two

1. Dye, D. A., Reck, M., & McDaniel, M. A. (1993). The validity of job knowledge measures. *International Journal of Selection and Assessment, 1*, 153–157.
2. Quinones, M. A., Ford, J. K., & Teachout, M. S. (1995). The relationship between work experience and job performance: A conceptual and meta-analytic review. *Personnel Psychology, 48*, 887–910.
3. Dokko, G., Wilk, S. L., & Rothbard, N. P. (2009). Unpacking prior experience: How career history affects job performance. *Organization Science, 20*(1), 51–68.
4. Society for Human Resource Management. (2011). *Background checking: Conducting reference background checks.* Alexandria, VA: Author; Dokko et al. (2009).
5. Moroney, R., & Carey, P. (2011). *Industry versus task-based experience and auditor performance.* Working paper, AFAANZ Conference, Gold Coast.
6. Housman, M. (2012). *Does previous work history predict future employment outcomes?* San Francisco, CA: Evolv.
7. Weekley, J. (2009). *Biodata: A tried and true means of predicting success.* Wayne, PA: Kenexa.
8. Bliesener, T. (1996). Methodological moderators in validating biographical data in personnel selection. *Journal of Occupational and Organizational Psychology, 69*, 107–120; Barge, B. N., & Hough, L. M. (1986). *Utility of biographical data for predicting job performance.* In L. M. Hough (Ed.), *Utility of temperament, biodata and interest assessment for predicting job performance: A review and integration of the literature.* Alexandra, VA: Army Research Institute; Manley, G. C., Benavidez, J., & Dunn, K. (2006). Development of a personality biodata measure to predict ethical decision making. *Journal of Managerial Psychology, 22*(7), 664–682.
9. Bobko, P., & Roth, P. L. (1999). Derivation and implications of a meta-analytic matrix incorporating cognitive ability, alternative predictors, and job performance. *Personnel Psychology, 52*, 561–589; Reilly, R. R., & Chao, G. T. (1982). Validity and fairness of some alternative employee selection procedures. *Personnel Psychology, 35*, 1–62.

10. McClelland, D. (1973). Testing for competence rather than intelligence. *American Psychologist, 28,* 1–14.

11. Semadar, A., Robins, G., & Ferris, G. R. (2006). Comparing the validity of multiple social effectiveness constructs in the prediction of managerial job performance. *Journal of Organizational Behavior, 27,* 443–461.

12. Bolden, R. (2010). Leadership competencies: Time to change the tune? *Leadership, 2*(2), 147–163.

13. Hollenbeck, G. P. (2009). Executive selection—what's right . . . what's wrong. *Industrial and Organizational Psychology, 2,* 130–143.

14. Smith, B., & Rutigliano, T. (2003). *Discover your sales strengths: How the world's greatest salespeople develop winning careers.* New York, NY: Warner Business Books.

15. Hunter, J. E., & Hunter, R. F. (1984). Validity and utility of alternative predictors of job performance. *Psychological Bulletin, 96,* 72–98.

16. Schmidt, F. L. (2002). The role of general cognitive ability and job performance: Why there cannot be a debate. *Human Performance, 15*(1/2), 187–210.

17. Dragoni, L., Oh, I.-S., Vankatwyk, P., & Tesluk, P. E. (2011). Developing executive leaders: The relative contribution of cognitive ability, personality, and the accumulation of work experience in predicting strategic thinking competency. *Personnel Psychology, 64,* 829–864.

18. Schmidt, F. L. (2012). Cognitive tests used in selection can have content validity as well as criterion validity: A broader research review and implications for practice. *International Journal of Selection and Assessment, 20*(1), 1–13; Schmidt, F. L., Hunter, J. E., & Outerbridge, A. N. (2012). Impact of job experience and ability on job knowledge, work sample performance, and supervisory ratings of job performance. *Journal of Applied Psychology, 71,* 432–439.

19. Sellman, W. S., Born, D. H., Strickland, W. J., & Ross, J. J. (2011). *Selection and classification in the US military.* In J. L. Farr & N. T. Tippins (Eds.), *Handbook of employee selection.* New York, NY: Routledge.

20. Hauknecht, J. P., & Langevin, A. M. (2011). *Selection for service and sales jobs*. In J. L. Farr & N. T. Tippins (Eds.), *Handbook of employee selection*. New York, NY: Routledge.

21. Nathan, B. R., & Alexander, R. A. (1998). A comparison of criteria for test validation: A meta-analytical investigation. *Personnel Psychology, 41,* 517–535.

22. DuBois, C.L.Z., Sackett, P. R., Zedeck, S., & Fogli, L. (1993). Further exploration of typical and maximum performance criteria: Definitional issues, prediction, and white-black differences. *Journal of Applied Psychology, 78,* 205–211.

23. Hollenbeck. (2009).

24. Murphy, K., Cronin, B., & Tam, A. (2003). Controversy and consensus regarding the use of cognitive ability testing in organizations. *Journal of Applied Psychology, 88,* 660–671.

25. Ben-Hur, S., Kinley, N., & Jonsen, K. (2012). Coaching executive teams to reach better decisions. *Journal of Management Development, 31*(7), 711–723; Guion, R. M. (2011). *Employee selection: Musings about its past, present, and future*. In J. L. Farr & N. T. Tippins (Eds.), *Handbook of employee selection*. New York, NY: Routledge.

26. Wagner, R. K., & Sternberg, R. J. (1985). Practical intelligence in real world pursuits: The role of tacit knowledge. *Journal of Personality and Social Psychology, 49,* 436–458; Sternberg, R. J. (1988). *The triarchic mind: A new theory of human intelligence*. New York, NY: Penguin Books.

27. Jaques, E. (1956). *Measurement of responsibility: A study of work, payment and individual capacity*. Cambridge, MA: Harvard University Press.

28. Topor, D. J., Colarelli, S. M., & Han, K. (2007). Influences of traits and assessment methods on human resource practitioners' evaluations of job applicants. *Journal of Business and Psychology, 21*(3), 361–376.

29. Judge, T., Higgins, C. A., Thoresen, C. J., & Barrick, M. R. (1999). The Big Five personality traits, general mental ability, and career success across the life span. *Personnel Psychology, 52,* 651–652.

30. Ones, D. S., Dilchert, S., Viswesvaran, C., & Judge, T. A. (2007). In support of personality assessment in organizational settings. *Personnel Psychology, 60,* 995–1027.

31. Rynes, S. L., Brown, K. G., & Colbert, A. E. (2002). Seven common misconceptions about human resource practices: Research findings versus practitioner beliefs. *Academy of Management Executive, 16*(3), 92–103.

32. Cook, M. (2009). *Personnel selection: Adding value through people.* Chichester, West Sussex: Wiley.

33. Robertson, I. T., Baron, H., Gibbons, P., MacIvor, R., & Nyfield, G. (2000). Conscientiousness and managerial performance. *Journal of Occupational and Organizational Psychology, 73*(2), 171–181.

34. Tracey, J. B., Sturman, M. C., & Tews, M. J. (2007). Ability versus personality: Factors that predict employee job performance. *Cornell Quarterly, 48,* 313–322.

35. Robertson et al. (2000).

36. Heggestad, E. D., & Gordon, H. L. (2008). An argument for context-specific personality assessments. *Industrial and Organizational Psychology, 1,* 320–322.

37. McDaniel, M. A., Rothstein, H. R., & Whetzel, D. L. (2006). Publication bias: A case study of four test vendors. *Personnel Psychology, 59,* 927–953.

38. Hogan, J., & Ones, D. S. (1997). *Conscientiousness and integrity at work.* In R. Hogan, J. A. Johnson, & S. R. Briggs (Eds.), *Handbook of personality psychology.* San Diego, CA: Academic Press.

39. Hough, L., & Dilchert, S. (2011). *Personality: Its measurement and validity for employee selection.* In J. L. Farr & N. T. Tippins (Eds.), *Handbook of employee selection.* New York, NY: Routledge.

40. Hough, L. M., & Oswald, F. L. (2000). Personnel selection: Looking toward the future—remembering the past. *Annual Review Psychology, 51,* 631–664.

41. Saville, P., MacIver, R., Kurz, R., & Hopton, T. (2008). *Project Epsom: How valid is a questionnaire?* Jersey: Saville Consulting Group.

42. Lombardo, M. M., Ruderman, M. N., & McCauley, C. D. (1988). Explanations of success and derailment in upper-level management positions. *Journal of Business and Psychology, 2,* 199–216.

43. Finkelstein, S. M. (2003). *Why smart executives fail: And what you can learn from their mistakes.* New York, NY: Portfolio.

44. Posner, B. Z., Kouzes, J. M., & Schmidt, W. H. (1985). Shared values make a difference: An empirical test of corporate culture. *Human Resource Management, 24*(3), 293.

45. Ones, D. S., Viswesvaran, C., & Schmidt, F. L. (1993). Comprehensive meta-analysis of integrity test validities: Findings and implications for personnel selection and theories of job performance. *Journal of Applied Psychology, 78,* 679–703.

46. Marlowe, H. A. (1986). Social intelligence: Evidence for multidimensionality and construct independence. *Journal of Educational Psychology, 78,* 52–58; Ferris, G. R., Witt, L. A., & Hochwarter, W. A. (2001). The interaction of social skill and general mental ability on work outcomes. *Journal of Applied Psychology, 86,* 1075–1082; Semadar, A., Robins, G., & Ferris, G. R. (2006). Comparing the validity of multiple social effectiveness constructs in the prediction of managerial job performance. *Journal of Organizational Behavior, 27,* 443–461.

47. Van Rooy, D. L., & Viswesvaran, C. (2004). Emotional intelligence: A meta-analytic investigation of predictive validity and nomological net. *Journal of Vocational Behavior, 65*(1), 71–95; O'Boyle, E. H., Humphrey, R. H., Pollack, J. M., Hawver, T. H., & Story, P. A. (2010). The relationship between emotional intelligence and job performance: A meta-analysis. *Journal of Organizational Behavior, 32,* 788–818.

48. Payne, S. C., Youngcourt, S. S., & Beaubien, J. M. (2007). A meta-analytic examination of the goal orientation nomological net. *Journal of Applied Psychology, 92,* 128–150.

Chapter Three

1. Ones, D. S., Dilchert, S., Viswesvaran, C., & Judge, T. A. (1993). In support of personality assessment in organisational settings. *Personnel Psychology, 60,* 995–1027.

2. Schmidt, F. L., & Hunter, J. E. (1998). The validity and utility of selection methods in personnel psychology: Practical and theoretical implications of 85 years of research findings. *Psychological Bulletin, 124*(2), 262–274.

3. Zeidner, M., Matthews, G., & Roberts, R. D. (2009). *What we know about emotional intelligence: How it affects learning, work, relationships, and our mental health.* Cambridge, MA: MIT Press.

4. Schmidt, F. L. (2002). The role of general cognitive ability and job performance: Why there cannot be a debate. *Human Performance, 15*(1/2), 187–210.

5. Ready, D. A., Conger, J. A., & Hill, L. A. (2010). Are you a high potential? *Harvard Business Review, 88*(6), 78–84.

6. Dries, N., Vantilborgh, T., & Pepermans, R. (2012). The role of learning agility and career variety in the identification and development of high potential employees. *Personnel Review, 41*(3), 340–358.

7. Judge, T. A., & Kammeyer-Mueller, J. D. (2012). On the value of aiming high: The causes and consequences of ambition. *Journal of Applied Psychology, 97*(4), 758–775.

8. Cascio, W. F., & Fogli, L. (2010). *The business value of employee selection.* In J. L. Farr & N. T. Tippins (Eds.), *Handbook of employee selection.* New York, NY: Routledge.

9. Groysberg, B., McLean, A. N., & Nohria, N. (2006). Are leaders portable? *Harvard Business Review, 84*(5), 92–100.

10. Vicino, F. L., & Bass, B. M. (1978). Lifespace variables and managerial success. *Journal of Applied Psychology, 63*(1), 81–88.

11. Human Capital Institute. (2011). *Quality in talent selection: Finding the perfect fit.* Washington, DC: Author.

12. Hough, L., & Dilchert, S. (2011). *Personality: Its measurement and validity for employment selection.* In J. L. Farr & N. T. Tippins (Eds.), *Handbook of employee selection.* New York, NY: Routledge.

13. Hochwarter, W. A., Witt, L. A., & Kacmar, K. M. (2000). Perceptions of organizational politics as a moderator of the relationship between conscientiousness and job performance. *Journal of Applied Psychology, 85*(3), 472–478.

14. Judge, T. A., Piccolo, R. F., & Illies, R. (2004). The forgotten ones: A re-examination of consideration, initiating structure and leadership effectiveness. *Journal of Applied Psychology, 89*(1), 36–51.

15. Stogdill, R. M., & Bass, B. M. (1990). *Bass and Stogdill's handbook of leadership: Theory, research, and managerial applications* (3rd ed.). New York, NY: Free Press.

16. Kristof-Brown, A. L., Zimmerman, R. D., & Johnson, E. C. (2005). Consequences of individuals' fit at work: A meta-analysis of person-job, person-organisation, person-group, and person-supervisor fit. *Personnel Psychology, 58*(2), 281–342.

17. Edwards, J. R. (1991). *Person-job fit: A conceptual integration, literature review, and methodological critique.* In C. L. Cooper & I. T. Robertson (Eds.), *International Review of Industrial and Organisational Psychology, 6,* 283–357.

18. Sekiguchi, T. (2004). Person-organization fit and person-job fit in employee selection: A review of the literature. *Osaka Keidai Ronshu, 54*(6), 179–196.

19. Kristof-Brown, A. L., Zimmerman, R. D., & Johnson, E. C. (2005). Consequences of individuals' fit at work: A meta-analysis of person-job, person-organisation, person-group, and person-supervisor fit. *Personnel Psychology, 58*(2), 281–342.

20. Vicino & Bass. (1978).

21. Mannix, E., & Neale, M. A. (2005). The influence of team monitoring on team processes and performance. *Human Performance, 17,* 25–41.

22. Bowers, C. A., Pharmer, J. A., & Salas, E. (2000). When member homogeneity is needed in work teams: A meta-analysis. *Small Group Research, 31*(1), 305.

23. Dokko, G., Wilk, S. L., & Rothbard, N. P. (2009). Unpacking prior experience: How career history affects job performance. *Organization Science, 20*(1), 51–68.

24. Cable, D. M., & Judge, T. A. (1997). Interviewers' perceptions of person-organization fit and organizational selection decisions. *Journal of Applied Psychology, 82*(4), 546–561.

25. Heggestad, E. D., & Gordon, H. L. (2008). An argument for context-specific personality assessments. *Industrial and Organizational Psychology, 1,* 320–322.

Chapter Four

1. Dudning, D., Heath, C., & Suls, J. M. (2003). Flawed self-assessment: Implications of health, education, and the workplace. *Psychological Science in the Public Interest, 5,* 69–106.

2. John, O. P., & Robins, R. W. (1994). Accuracy and bias in self-perception: Individual differences in self-enhancement and the role of narcissism. *Journal of Personality and Social Psychology, 66*(1), 206–219.

3. Kruger, J., & Dunning, D. (1999). Unskilled and unaware of it: How difficulties in recognizing one's own incompetence lead to inflated self-assessments. *Journal of Personality and Social Psychology, 77*(6), 1121–1134.

4. Paulhus, D. L., & Reid, D. B. (1991). Enhancement and denial in socially desirable responding. *Journal of Personality and Social Psychology, 60,* 307–317.

5. Crandall, J. E. (1973). Sex differences in extreme response style: Differences in frequency of extreme positive and negative ratings. *Journal of Social Psychology, 89,* 281–293.

6. Gentry, W. A., Yip, J., & Hannum, K. M. (2010). Self-observer rating discrepancies of managers in Asia: A study of derailment characteristics and behaviors in southern and Confucian Asia. *International Journal of Selection and Assessment, 18*(3), 237–250; Eckert, R., Ekelund, B. Z., Gentry, W. A., & Dawson, J. F. (2010). "I don't see me like you see me, but is that a problem?" Cultural influences on rating discrepancy in 360-degree feedback instruments. *European Journal of Work and Organizational Psychology, 19*(3), 259–278.

7. Rosenzweig, P. (2007). *The halo effect: . . . and the eight other business delusions that deceive managers.* New York, NY: Simon & Schuster.

8. Bernthal, P. R., & Wellins, R. S. (2005). *Leadership forecast 2005/2006: Best practices for tomorrow's global leaders.* Pittsburgh, PA: Development Dimensions International.

9. Eichinger, R. W., & Lombardo, M. M. (2004). Patterns of rater accuracy in 360-degree. *Perspectives, 27,* 23–25.

10. Antonioni, D., & Park, J. (2001). The effects of personality similarity on peer ratings of contextual work behaviors. *Personnel Psychology, 54,* 331–360.

11. Khaneman, D. (2011). *Thinking, fast and slow.* London: Penguin Books.

12. MacKinnon, R. A. (2010). *Assessment and Talent Management Survey 2010.* Thame, Oxon: TalentQ.

13. Fallaw, S. S., Kantrowitz, T. M., & Dawson, C. R. (2012). *Global assessment trends report*. Thames Ditton, Surrey: DHL Group.

14. Chartered Institute of Personnel and Development. (2011). *Resourcing and talent planning*. Annual survey report. London: Author.

15. Cortina, J. M., Goldstein, N. B., Payne, S. C., Kristl-Davison, H., & Gilliland, S. W. (2000). The incremental validity of interview scores over and above cognitive ability and conscientiousness. *Personnel Psychology, 53*(2), 325–351.

16. Ryan, A. M., & Sackett, P. R. (1989). Exploratory study of individual assessment practices: Interrater reliability and judgments of assessor effectiveness. *Journal of Applied Psychology, 74*(4), 568–579.

17. Salgado, J. F., & Moscoso, S. (2002). Comprehensive meta analysis of the construct validity of the employment interview. *European Journal of Work and Organizational Psychology, 11*(3), 299–324.

18. Campion, M. A., Palmer, D. K., & Campion, J. E. (1997). A review of structure in the selection interview. *Personnel Psychology, 50*, 655–702.

19. Huffcutt, A. I., & Arthur, W. Jr. (1994). Hunter & Hunter (1984) revisited: Interview validity for entry-level jobs. *Journal of Applied Psychology, 79*, 184–190; Wiesner, W. H., & Cronshaw, S. F. (1988). The moderating impact of interview format and degree of structure on interview validity. *Journal of Occupational Psychology, 61*, 275–290.

20. Cook, M. (2009). *Personnel selection: Adding value through people*. Chichester, West Sussex: Wiley; Terpstra, D. E., Mohamed, A. A., & Kethley, R. B. (1999). An analysis of federal court cases involving nine selection cases. *International Journal of Selection and Assessment, 7*, 26–34.

21. Campion, M. A., & Campion, J. E. (1994). Structured interviewing: A note on incremental validity and alternative question types. *Journal of Applied Psychology, 79*(6), 998–1002.

22. Salgado, J. F., & Moscoso, S. (2002). Comprehensive meta analysis of the construct validity of the employment interview. *European Journal of Work and Organizational Psychology, 11*(3), 299–324.

23. Rynes, S., & Gerhart, B. (1990). Interview assessments of appli-
    cant "fit": An exploratory investigation. *Personnel Psychology, 43,*
    13–35.

24. Oh, I. S., Postlethwaite, B. E., Schmidt, F. L., McDaniel, M. A., &
    Whetzel, D. L. (2007). *Do structured and unstructured interviews have
    near equal validity? Implications of recent developments in meta-analysis.*
    Paper presented at the 22nd Annual Conference of the Society for
    Industrial and Organizational Psychology, New York, NY.

25. Silzer, R., & Jeanneret, R. (2011). Individual psychological assess-
    ment: A practice and science in search of a common ground. *Indus-
    trial and Organisational Psychology, 4,* 270–296.

26. Ben-Hur, S., & Kinley, N. (2012). Coaching executive teams to
    better decisions. *Journal of Management Development, 31*(7),
    711–723.

27. Lievens, F., Highhouse, S., & De Corte, W. (2005). The impor-
    tance of traits and abilities in supervisors' hirability decisions as a
    function of method of assessment. *Journal of Occupational and
    Organizational Psychology, 78,* 453–470.

28. Hogan, R. (2005). In defense of personality measurement: New
    wine for old whiners. *Human Performance, 18*(4), 331–341.

29. Mead, A. D., & Drasgow, F. (1993). Effects of administration
    medium: A meta-analysis. *Psychological Bulletin, 114,* 449–458.

30. Hughes, D., & Tate, L. (2007). To cheat or not to cheat: Candi-
    dates' perceptions and experiences of unsupervised computer-
    based testing. *Selection and Development Review, 23,* 13–18.

31. Burke, E. (2006). *Better practice for unsupervised online assessment.*
    London: SHL Group.

32. Connelly, B. S., & Ones, D. S. (2008). Inter-rater reliability in
    assessment centre ratings: A meta-analysis. Paper presented at
    23rd Annual Conference of the Society for Industrial and Orga-
    nizational Psychology, San Francisco.

33. Gaugler, B. B., Rosenthal, D. B., Thornton, G. C., & Bentson, C.
    (1987). Meta-analysis of assessment center validity. *Journal of
    Applied Psychology, 72*(3), 493–511.

34. Lance, C. (2008). Why assessment centers do not work the way
    they are supposed to. *Industrial and Organizational Psychology, 1*(1),
    84–97.

35. Thornton, G. C., & Gibbons, A. M. (2009). Validity of assessment centers for personnel selection. *Human Resource Management Review, 19*, 169–187.

36. Eurich, T. L., Krause, D. E., Cigularov, K., & Thornton III, G. C. (2009). Assessment centers: Current practices in the United States. *Journal of Business Psychology, 24*, 387–407.

37. McDaniel, M. A., & Nguyen, N. T. (2001). Situational judgment tests: A review of practice and constructs assessed. *International Journal of Selection and Assessment, 9*, 103–113.

38. McDaniel, M. A., Hartman, N. S., Whetzel, D. L., & Grubb, W. L. (2007). Situational judgment tests, response instructions, and validity: A meta-analysis. *Personnel Psychology, 60*, 63–91.

39. McDaniel, M. A., Morgeson, F. P., Finnegan, E. B., Campion, M. A., & Braverman, E. P. (2001). Use of situational judgment tests to predict job performance: A clarification of the literature. *Journal of Applied Psychology, 86*, 730–740.

40. McDaniel et al. (2007).

41. Roller, R. L., & Morris, S. B. (2008). Individual assessment: Meta-analysis. In I. L. Kwaske (Chair). *Individual assessment: Does the research support the practice?* Symposium presented at the 23rd Annual Conference of the Society for Industrial Organizational Psychology, San Francisco, CA.

42. Prien, E. P., Schippmann, J. S., & Prien, K. O. (2003). *Individual assessment: As practiced in industry and consulting.* Mahwah, NJ: Erlbaum.

43. Fletcher, C. (2011). Individual psychological assessments in organisations: Big in practice, short on evidence? *Assessment and Development Matters, 3*(2), 23–26.

44. Ryan, A. M., & Sackett, P. R. (1998). *Individual assessment: The research base.* In R. Jeanneret & R. Silzer (Eds.), *Individual psychological assessment: Predicting behavior in organizational settings.* San Francisco, CA: Jossey-Bass.

45. McEvoy, G. M., & Beatty, R. W. (1989). Assessment centers and subordinate appraisals of managers: A seven year examination of predictive validity. *Personnel Psychology, 42*(1), 37–52.

46. Rehbine, N. (2007). *The impact of 360-degree feedback on leadership development.* Unpublished doctoral dissertation, Capella University, Minneapolis.

47. Jawahar, I. M., & Williams, C. R. (1997). Where all the children are above average: A meta-analysis of the performance appraisal. *Personnel Psychology, 50*(4), 905–925.

48. Eichinger, R. W., & Lombardo, M. M. (2004). Patterns of rater accuracy in 360-degree. *Perspectives, 27,* 23–25.

49. Kaiser, R. B., & Kaplan, R. E. (2005). Overlooking overkill? Beyond the 1-to-5 rating scale. *Human Resources Planning, 28*(3), 7–11.

50. Yammarino, F. J., & Atwater, L. E. (1997). Do managers see themselves as others see them? Implications of self-other rating agreement for human resources management. *Organizational Dynamics, 25*(4), 35–44.

51. Roth, P. L., Bobko, P., & McFarland, L. A. (2005). A meta-analysis of work sample test validity. *Personnel Psychology, 58,* 1009–1037.

Chapter Five

1. Ryan, A., Mcfarland, L., Baron, H., & Page, R. (1999). An international look at selection practices. *Personnel Psychology, 52,* 359–362.

2. König, C. J., Klehe, U. C., Berchtold, M., & Kleinmann, M. (2010). Reasons for being selective when choosing personnel selection procedures. *International Journal of Selection and Assessment, 18,* 17–27.

3. Huo, Y. P., Huang, H. J., & Napier, N. K. (2002). Divergence or convergence: A cross-national comparison of personnel selection practices. *Human Resource Management, 41,* 31–44.

4. Tyler, G., Newcombe, P., & Barrett, P. (2005). The Chinese challenge to the Big-5. *Selection and Development Review, 21*(6), 10–14.

5. Stagner, R. (1957). Some problems in contemporary industrial psychology. *Bulletin of the Menninger Clinic, 21,* 238–247.

6. Tracey, J. B., Sturman, M. C., & Tews, M. J. (2007). Ability versus personality: Factors that predict employee job performance. *Cornell Quarterly, 48,* 313–322.

7. Fallaw, S. W., & Kantrowitz, T. M. (2011). *Global assessment trends report.* Thames Ditton, Surrey: SHL.

8. Hausknecht, J. P., Day, D. V., & Thomas, S. C. (2004). Applicant reactions to selection procedures: An updated model and meta-analysis. *Personnel Psychology, 57*, 639–683; Smither, J. W., Reilly, R. R., Millsap, R. E., Pearlman, K., & Stoffey, R. (1993). Applicant reactions to selection procedures. *Personnel Psychology, 46*, 49–76.

9. Hausknecht et al. (2004); Walsh, B. M., Tuller, M. D., Barnes-Farrell, J. L., & Matthews, R. A. (2010). Investigating the moderating role of cultural practices on the effect of selection fairness perceptions. *International Journal of Selection and Assessment, 18*(4), 366–379; Anderson, N., Ahmed, S., & Costa, A. C. (2012). Applicant reactions in Saudi Arabia: Organizational attractiveness and core-self-evaluation. *International Journal of Selection and Assessment, 20*, 197–208.

10. Gilliland, S. W. (1995). Fairness from the applicant's perspective: Reactions to employee selection procedures. *International Journal of Selection and Assessment, 3*, 11–19.

11. Erker, S., & Buczynski, K. (2009). *Are you failing the interview: Survey of global interviewing practices and perceptions.* Pittsburgh, PA: Developmental Dimensions International.

12. Sumanth, J. J., & Cable, D. M. (2011). Status and organizational entry: How organizational and individual status affect justice perceptions of hiring systems. *Personnel Psychology, 64*, 963–1000.

13. Jones, S. (2011). The good, the bad and the ugly: A review of job candidate experiences of psychological testing. *Assessment and Development Matters, 3*(1), 5–6.

14. Bauer, T. N., Maert, C. P., Dolen, M. R., & Campion, M. A. (1998). Longitudinal assessment of applicant reactions to employment testing and testing outcome feedback. *Journal of Applied Psychology, 83*, 892–903.

15. Sacket, P. R., Shen, W., et al. (2011). Perspectives from twenty-two countries on the legal environment for selection. In J. L. Farr & N. T. Tippins (Eds.), *Handbook of employee selection.* New York, NY: Routledge.

16. te Nijenhuis, J., de Jong, M., Evers, A., & van der Flier, H. (2004). Are cognitive differences between immigrants and majority groups diminishing? *European Journal of Personality, 18*, 405–434.

17. Fontaine, J.R.J., Schittekatte, M., Groenvynck, H., & De Clercq, S. (2006). *Acculturation and intelligence among Turkish and Moroccan adolescents in Belgium*. Unpublished manuscript, Ghent University.

18. Chan, D., & Hough, L. (2011). Categories of individual difference constructs for employee selection. In J. L. Farr & N. T. Tippins (Eds.), *Handbook of employee selection*. New York, NY: Routledge.

19. Hausdorf, P. A., LeBlanc, M. M., & Chawla, A. (2003). Cognitive ability testing and employment selection: Does test content relate to adverse impact? *Applied HRM Research, 7*(2), 41–48.

20. Huffcutt, A. I., & Roth, P. L. (1998). Racial group differences in employment interview evaluations. *Journal of Applied Psychology, 83,* 179–189; Bobko, P., Roth, P. L., & Potosky, D. (1999). Derivation and implications of a meta-analysis matrix incorporating cognitive ability, alternative predictors, and job performance. *Personnel Psychology. 52,* 561–589; Goldstein, H. W., Yusko, K. P., & Nicolopoulos, V. (2001). Exploring black-white subgroup differences of managerial competencies. *Personnel Psychology, 54,* 783–808.

21. Pyburn, K. M. Jr., Ployhart, R. E., & Kravitz, D. A. (2008). The diversity-validity dilemma: Overview and legal context. *Personnel Psychology, 61,* 143–151.

22. Thanks to Steve O'Dell of TalentQ for this tip.

23. McDaniel, M. A., Hartman, N. S., Whetzel, D. S., & Grubb, W. L. (2007). Situational judgment tests, response instructions, and validity: a meta-analysis. *Personnel Psychology, 60,* 63–91.

24. Ryan, A. M., Ployhart, R. E., & Friedel, L. A. (1998). Using personality testing to reduce adverse impact: A cautionary tale. *Journal of Applied Psychology, 83*(2), 298–307.

25. Steele, C. M., & Aronson, J. (1995). Stereotype threat and the intellectual test performance of African Americans. *Journal of Personality and Social Psychology, 69*(5), 797–811.

26. Sackett, P. R., Hardison, C. M., & Cullen, M. J. (2004). On the value of correcting mischaracterizations of stereotype threat research. *American Psychologist, 59*(1), 48–49.

27. Avolio, B. J., & Waldman, D. A. (1994). Variation in cognitive, perceptual, and psychomotor abilities across the working life span:

Examining the effects of race, sex, experience, education, and occupational type. *Psychology and Aging, 9,* 430–442.

28. Specht, J., Egloff, B., & Schmukle, S. C. (2011). Stability and change of personality across the life course: The impact of age and major life events on mean-level and rank-order stability of the Big Five. *Journal of Personality and Social Psychology, 101*(4), 862–882.

29. Tett, R. P., Fitzke, J. R., Wadlington, P. L., Davies, S. A., Anderson, M. G., & Foster, J. (2009). The use of personality test norms in work settings: Effects of sample size and relevance. *Journal of Occupational and Organisational Psychology, 82,* 639–659.

30. Chartered Institute of Personnel and Development. (2011). *Resourcing and talent planning.* Annual survey report. London: Author.

Chapter Six

1. Lawton, D. (2012). Personal communication. Cubiks, Ltd.
2. MacKinnon, R. A. (2010). *Assessment and Talent Management Survey.* Thame, Oxfordshire: Talent Q.
3. Tippins, N. (2012). Personal communication.
4. Ployhart, R. E., Ryan, A. M., & Bennett, M. (1999). Explanations for selection decisions: Applicants' reactions to informational and sensitivity features of explanations. *Journal of Applied Psychology, 84*(1), 87–106.
5. Murphy, K. R. (2008). Perspectives on the relationship between job performance and ratings of job performance. *Industrial and Organizational Psychology, 1,* 197–205.
6. Grote, D. (2005). *Forced ranking: Making performance management work.* Boston, MA: Harvard Business Press.
7. Borman, W. C., Bryant, R. H., & Dorio, J. (2011). *The measurement of task performance as criteria in selection research.* In J. L. Farr & N. T. Tippins (Eds.), *Handbook of employee selection.* New York, NY: Routledge.
8. Borman, W. C., Penner, L. A., Allen, T. D., & Motowidlo, S. J. (2001). Personality predictors of citizenship performance. *International Journal of Selection and Assessment, 9,* 52–69.

9. Borman, W. C., Bryant, R. H., & Dorio, J. (2011). *The measurement of task performance as criteria in selection research.* In J. L. Farr & N. T. Tippins (Eds.), *Handbook of employee selection.* New York, NY: Routledge.

10. Brockett, J. (2012, June 18). Mining firm uses "seven second" appraisal forms. *People Management Online.* Retrieved September 14, 2012, from www.peoplemanagement.co.uk/pm/articles/2012/06/mining-firm-uses-seven-second-appraisal-forms.htm?utm_medium=email&utm_source=cipd&utm_campaign=pmdaily_190612&utm_content=news_3

11. Organ, D. W. (1988). *Organizational citizenship behavior: The good soldier syndrome.* Lexington, MA: Lexington Books; Brief, A. P., & Motowidlo, S. J. (1986). Prosocial organizational behaviors. *Academy of Management Review, 11,* 710–725; Van Dyne, L., Cummings, L. L., & McLean-Parks, J. (1995). Extra role behaviors: In pursuit of construct and definitional clarity (a bridge over muddied waters). *Research in Organizational Behavior, 17,* 215–285; Borman, W. C., & Motowidlo, S. J. (1993). *Expanding the criterion domain to include elements of contextual performance.* In N. Schmitt & W. C. Borman (Eds.), *Personnel selection in organizations.* San Francisco, CA: Jossey-Bass.

Chapter Seven

1. Saville, P. (2011). Personal communication.

2. Hurtz, G. M., & Donovan, J. J. (2000). Personality and job performance: The Big Five revisited. *Journal of Applied Psychology, 85,* 869–879.

3. Barrick, M. R., & Mount, M. K. (1993). Autonomy as a moderator of the relationships between the Big Five personality dimensions and job performance. *Journal of Applied Psychology, 78,* 111–118.

4. Witt L. A., Burke, L. A., Barrick, M. R., & Mount, M. K. (2002). The interactive effects of conscientiousness and agreeableness on job performance. *Journal of Applied Psychology, 87*(1), 164–169.

5. Meehl, P. E. (1954). *Clinical versus statistical prediction: A theoretical analysis and a review of the evidence.* Lanham, MD: Rowan & Littlefield/Jason Aronson. (Original work published 1954).

6. MacKinnon, R. A. (2010). *Assessment and talent management survey*. Thame, Oxfordshire: Talent Q.
7. Fernández-Aráoz, C. (2005). Getting the right people at the top. *MIT Sloan Management Review, 46(4)*, 67–72.
8. Manyika, J., Chui, M., Brown, B., Bughin, J., Dobbs, R., Roxburgh, C., & Hung Byers, A.(2011). *Big data: The next frontier for innovation, competition, and productivity*. New York, NY: McKinsey.
9. Roch, S. G., Woehr, D. J., Mishra, V., & Kieszczynska, U. (2012). Rater training revisited: An updated meta-analytic review of frame-of-reference training. *Journal of Occupational and Organizational Psychology, 85*, 370–395.

Chapter Eight

1. Klaas, B. S., McClendon, J., & Gainey, T. W. (1999). HR outsourcing and its impact: The role of transaction costs. *Personnel Psychology, 52(1)*, 113–136.
2. Enlow, S., & Ertel, D. (2006). Achieving outsourcing success: Effective relationship management. *Compensation and Benefits Review, 38*, 50–55.

Appendix

1. Saville, P., MacIver, R., Kurz, R., & Hopton, T. (2008, January). *Project Epsom: How valid is a questionnaire?* Jersey: Saville Consulting Group. Conference, Stratford-upon-Avon.
2. Cook, M. (2009). *Personnel selection: Adding value through people*. Chichester, West Sussex: Wiley.
3. Arthur, W., & Bennett, W. (1995). The international assignee: The relative importance of factors perceived to contribute to success. *Personnel Psychology, 48*, 99–114.
4. Mol, S. T., Born, M. P., Willemsen, M. E., & Van der Molen, H. T. (2005). Predicting expatriate job performance for selection purposes: A quantitative review. *Journal of Cross-Cultural Psychology, 36*, 590–620.

5. Bhaskar-Shrinivas, P., Harrison, D. A., Shaffer, M. A., & Luk, D. M. (2005). Input-based and time-based models of international adjustment: Meta-analytic evidence and theoretical extensions. *Academy of Management Journal, 48,* 257–281.

6. Black, J. S., & Stephens, G. K. (1989). The influence of the spouse on American expatriate adjustment and intent to stay in Pacific Rim overseas assignments. *Journal of Management, 15*(4), 529–544.

7. Arthur & Bennett. (1995).

8. Ones, D. S., Viswesvaran, C., & Schmidt, F. L. (1993). Comprehensive meta-analysis of integrity test validities: Findings and implications for personnel selection and theories of job performance. *Journal of Applied Psychology, 78,* 679–703.

9. Ones, D. S., Viswesvaran, C., & Schmidt, F. L. (1993). Comprehensive meta-analysis of integrity test validities: Findings and implications for personnel selection and theories of job performance. *Journal of Applied Psychology, 78,* 679–703.

10. Salgado, J. F. (2002). The Big Five personality dimensions and counterproductive behaviours. *International Journal of Selection and Assessment, 10,* 117–125.

11. Van Iddekinge, C. H., Roth, P. L., Raymark, P. H., & Odle-Dusseau, H. N. (2012). The criterion-related validity of integrity tests: An updated meta-analysis. *Journal of Applied Psychology, 97*(3), 499–530.

12. Ones, D. S., Viswesvaran, C., & Schmidt, F. L. (1993). Comprehensive meta-analysis of integrity test validities: Findings and implications for personnel selection and theories of job Performance. *Journal of Applied Psychology, 78,* 679–703.

13. Berry, C. M., Sackett, P. R., & Wiemann, S. (2007). A review of recent developments in integrity test research. *Personnel Psychology, 60,* 271–301.

14. Huiras, J., Uggen, C., & McMorris, B. (2000). Career jobs, survival jobs, and employee deviance: A social investment model of workplace misconduct. *Sociological Quarterly, 41,* 245–263.

15. Hershcovis, M. S., Turner, N., Barling, J., Arnold, K. A., Dupré, K. E., Inness, M., LeBlanc, M. M., & Sivanathan, N. (2007).

Predicting workplace aggression: A meta-analysis. *Journal of Applied Psychology, 92,* 228–238.

16. Cook. (2009).

17. Avolio, B. J., & Waldman, D. A. (1994). Variation in cognitive, perceptual, and psychomotor abilities across the working life span: Examining the effects of race, sex, experience, education, and occupational type. *Psychology and Aging, 9,* 430–442.

18. Saville et al. (2008).

Index

t represents table.